FOUR MILES EAST OF
BAGDAD

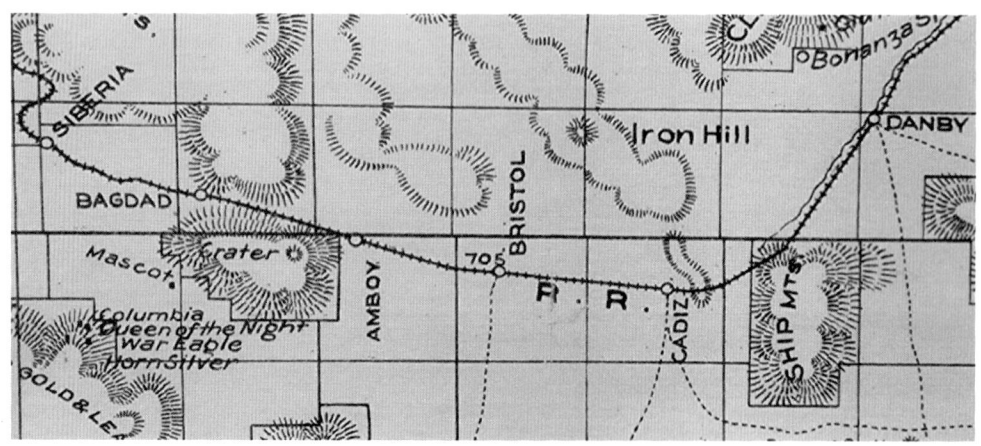

STEVE REYES

FOUR MILES EAST OF
BAGDAD

Crime, Violence and the Railroad in
San Bernardino County, California 1896-1897

PALMETTO
PUBLISHING
Charleston, SC
www.PalmettoPublishing.com

Paperback ISBN: 979-8-8229-5127-3

Courtesy of the Needles Historical Society
(Photo of the Mexican "Big Hat Brigade" labor force circa 1900)

Courtesy of the San Bernardino County Museum
(Photo of Train Coming Into Bagdad and Exterior of Harvey House)

Courtesy of the San Bernardino County Assessor Recorder's Office
(Photo of Louis James Searcy circa 1897)

FOR THE FORGOTTEN AND
TROUBLED SOULS BURIED
AT GHOST SETTLEMENTS IN
THE GREAT MOJAVE DESERT

CONTENTS

FOREWORD

I have always had a love for adventure, especially in deserts, and I have been fortunate to have shared many back-road adventures in the Mojave Desert with Steve Reyes and his wife and have fond memories of watching the sunset from the back patio of their home. So when Steve told me of a tragedy that he had read about—a story of a murder and probable injustice that happened 125 years ago in a remote area of the desert—I could sense the interest in his voice, and I knew that because of Steve's law-enforcement background, he would be all too anxious to dig into the details of a story like this one. I was not disappointed.

In the late 1800s and early 1900s, steam engines required watering stops along the railroad tracks about every nine miles, and these sites were occupied by small groups of workers, some of whom had families living in section houses. In these settlements, small businesses, mostly saloons, also sprang up, and these railroad watering stops, remote and primitive, naturally attracted a criminal element—hobos, tramps, and other ne'er-do-wells following the tracks and looking for handouts or any opportunity to rob or steal. Life in these remote desert communities was rough and sometimes brutal. This true story centers on one such settlement—Bagdad, California.

The desert is quiet now. Homes and businesses that once bordered Route 66 through the Mojave Desert have long since been abandoned, and most have succumbed to the elements and are either entirely gone or are simply faint outlines of concrete foundations. Likewise, when the railroad switched from steam engines to diesel locomotives beginning in the mid-1930s, the train depots and watering stops became unnecessary, the section houses were demolished, workers left, and the sites were abandoned. Today, there is only a single tree and an obscure cemetery to mark where Bagdad once stood.

In 1896 a murder took place on the railroad tracks east of Bagdad, and the story of the rush to justice in the trial of one man who was thought to be the culprit, defended by youthful attorneys just out of law school, makes for a fascinating read. Steve has done an amazing amount of research tracking down all the pieces of this story and has spent hours in archives and museums poring over investigative documents—trial transcripts, court records, prison records, newspaper accounts, and secondary source materials, all of which date to the late 1800s and early 1900s.

This is a story that could only be written by an author with Steve's extensive experience of the inner workings of courts and law-enforcement procedures and with his comprehensive understanding of justice, forgiveness, and truth.

Joe de Kehoe
Estes Park, Colorado
Author: *The Silence and the Sun*

On July 27, 1866, an act of Congress chartered construction of the Atlantic and Pacific Railroad with the vision of creating a line from Springfield, Missouri, to the Pacific Ocean. In 1883 the construction of the railroad reached the uninhabited and desolate Mojave Desert between Needles and Barstow in San Bernardino County, California. Chinese laborers completed much of the hard labor and moved on after completion, and the ensuing locomotive traffic created an insatiable appetite for manpower. Men were needed to service the tracks and locomotives and provide coal and water for the engines. The nature of the steam engine required water replenishment approximately every nine miles. Small settlements or sidings, which consisted of section houses and shacks, were constructed to provide shelter. Contract laborers were not considered employees and typically built their own shelter from discarded railroad ties. The sidings were named alphabetically: Amboy, Bagdad, Cadiz, Danby, Edison, Fenner, Goffs, Homer, Ibex, and Java. The population of the smallest settlements was approximately ten, while Bagdad's swelled to as high as thirty to forty, based on labor needs.[1] With the advent of automobiles and the establishment of Route 66, many of the stops along the Mother Road took on the names of these sidings.

Bagdad, the midpoint between Needles and Barstow, is situated at the base of a large grade. Amboy Crater, and its ancient lava flow, sits four miles to the east and is a geological wonder. In 1896 Bagdad was home to a Harvey House lunch counter where passing travelers and railroad employees could eat, a railroad station, a telegraph office, an icehouse, a few large water tanks, several large homes, bunkhouses, and a large building that housed an illegal saloon. Outhouses or washhouses dotted the landscape, and there was a corral behind the saloon where passing travelers could leave their horses while they drank. The telegraph allowed for instantaneous communication with San Bernardino.

In 1882 there was mass immigration to America, with 788,992 new arrivals. San Bernardino County was in flux as everyone was in transit and in transition.[2] The population of these settlements reflected the ethnicities, societal norms, and transient nature of the United States. Irish, German, Mexican, French, Native American, Japanese, and Chinese worked together with the common mission of supporting the railroad. Different languages and accents were found at these settlements, and railroad employees tended to move on after a short time. Mexican contract laborers replaced Chinese laborers on the western lines, finding work and temporary homes in Bagdad.[3] The Mexicans segregated themselves in an area built of shacks and tie houses, based on their comfort in being around other laborers with a common culture and language. The Caucasian population rarely visited this area of Bagdad and called it Chihuahua, going there only out of necessity.

Workers had titles such as section hand, section boss, and track-walker. Their only responsibility was their section of tracks, which typically ran nine miles. The work crews of four to five men started their work in one direction before returning to their respective settlements, where they lived during their employment. The work crews serviced the line as marked by the trackwalker and replaced broken bolts, broken straps, and damaged rails.

The day started with the ringing of a bell by the keeper of the bunkhouse, typically the wife of an employee, followed by breakfast for sale at the cost of twenty-five cents. After breakfast the work crews gathered their tools and loaded them onto a handcar, which was the mainstay along the railroad. Despite nostalgic and romanticized visions of travel on horseback, the primary mode of transportation while working on the line was the handcar. To avoid a collision with an oncoming train, the handcars were lifted and removed from the tracks by the crew. The work along these railroad sections was dangerous, laborious, and monotonous, and the crews worked back and forth along their section of tracks.

Traveling on foot along the rails before seven o'clock in the morning and in the opposite direction of the work crews meant you were unaware of the work schedule or potential perils of traveling alone in the remote desert. Indeed, a peculiar facet of life in Bagdad was the importance of time. The train schedule dictated when the workers ate and left for work and when the trains came and went. At exactly 6:15 a.m., meals were served to workers at a cost; by 7:00 a.m. the track workers and work crews left for the day.

Train crashes, derailments, and explosions caused the loss of fingers and limbs, and death was not uncommon. If you chose to work around the railroad, you had a 20 percent chance of being killed at work.[4] And everything had to be freighted in at a charge, which increased the cost of food and housewares. This led to a poorly balanced diet consisting of canned beans and salt pork with a lack of fresh fruit and vegetables. Constipation and stomach ailments were common, and a lack of understanding about the need for a balanced diet made life that much more uncomfortable for the residents of Bagdad. Food was often contaminated, and typhoid, dysentery, and diarrhea were common.[5] Water brought in by train was stored in large water tanks and drank by the locals. Trips to the outhouse or washhouse were common, and the facilities consisted of a shallow hole in the ground covered by a wooden structure. Opium was a common treatment for stomach ailments; it could be found in elixirs and was used to treat many of the maladies suffered by the residents living at remote railroad settlements.[6] The readily available vice at Bagdad was alcohol, which came in the form of whiskey, beer, and wine.

In 1896 the economy was slowly awakening from the Panic of 1893, a terrible depression that lasted four years. By 1894 four million men out of a population of sixty-five million were seeking work. There would not be a worse depression until the 1930s.[7] The labor force along the railroad was constantly moving, and "vagrants, squatters, and regiments of unemployed workers took to the roads."[8] This population of unemployed laborers were referred to as "tramps" or "hobos."

The arrest logs of the San Bernardino County Sheriff's Department were filled with arrests for vagrancy and the ensuing jail sentences of offenders. Arrests were made along the railroad at the far-off settlements, and the violating tramps were transported back to San Bernardino to complete their sentences. The sentence and transportation back to San Bernadino, far from their home states, ensured vagrants would quickly leave town after their release from county jail.

Most did not care about the expanse or beauty of the land; they had come to the desert for work and had no desire to stay leaving within a year or two of employment. The living desert wants to bite, poke, or stick in your body, and the weather is unforgiving. Often torrential rain falls in one area and less than a few miles away, the sun is shining in a cloudless sky. Flash floods can wipe away natural or man-made obstructions in seconds.

Death came in many ways, which included ever-present influenza, pneumonia, typhus, scarlet fever, measles, whooping cough, and tuberculosis. It is estimated that 35 to 40 percent of households would see the death of one of their children before the offspring left the home. In 1896 the average lifespan was forty-six years, and mortality and the fascination with death were part of the daily conversation of life in the United States. Death even made its way onto moving trains: passengers were sometimes found dead during routine stops. Victorian America remained an unhealthy and deadly place, and mortality was even higher among railroad settlement populations.[9]

County government is one of the oldest forms of local government and dates to medieval England. Outside of cities, counties are local political jurisdictions that deliver public services. The county acts as an administrator of the state, providing law enforcement, a court system, jailing of prisoners, elections, and the recording of births, marriages, and deaths. Services are minimal and overburdened, and this model remains unchanged today.

On April 26, 1853, the County of San Bernardino was created by a legislative act separating it from Los Angeles County. The act set forth the elections of the county judge, county attorney, county clerk, county surveyor, sheriff, coroner, treasurer, and assessor. The townships of Chino, San Salvador, and San Bernardino were created, and these townships were governed by commissioners until the board of supervisors was formed.

On April 13, 1854, the City of San Bernardino was selected as the county seat, and in March 1855, statutes of California made it mandatory for each county to have a board of supervisors. San Bernardino County was required to have three supervisors for three districts. On May 19, 1855, the first official meeting of the board was recorded; the first official items of business were the division of the county into five road districts and the appointment of a supervisor for each road district.[10] Later, the board of supervisors would grow to five board members.

When the railroads arrived, San Bernardino changed from a small western town into a thriving city. In 1883 the Southern Pacific arrived in Colton, and in 1885 the Sante Fe completed its line through the Cajon Pass into San Bernardino itself. As a result, thousands of visitors passed through San Bernadino, and many decided to stay. By 1886 there were hotels and business blocks; a stone courthouse was built in 1893 on the corner of Court and E Streets.[11] By the 1890s, San Bernardino was an important trade center and railroad town. The board of supervisors met at the county seat 150 miles away from Bagdad. The primary county services were law enforcement and the coroner.

By 1870, 80 percent of the total population of the United States was literate, which meant reading newspapers, magazines, and periodicals was popular. By the turn of the century, the circulation of daily, Sunday, and weekly newspapers increased to thirty-nine million, up from only seven million in 1870. In fact, the working-class American society had an insatiable appetite for reading, and in the 1870s, Old Sleuth dime-store crime novels were published. The fictional detective character, Old Sleuth, solved crimes and appealed to the less sophisticated working class with a desire for social order. The detective character operated independently and interacted with law enforcement only after apprehending the criminal. He was able to get himself out of any situation, no matter how dangerous. Harlan Page

Halsey, the author, was a businessman and member of the Brooklyn Board of Education who made quite a bit of money from royalties. The literature was mass-produced and made from the cheapest grade of paper, hence the name "pulp fiction." The cost of the novels ranged from one cent to fifteen cents, and they were intended to "excite, astonish, and arouse, providing readers sensationalism and escapism."[12] They were perfect reading material for the remote railroad settlements, where entertainment was nonexistent.

In 1896 an unsolved murder and the resulting quick-paced investigation offered a real-life dime-store-novel plot and captured the fascination of the community in San Bernardino. On December 6, 1896, Joseph Otto was found murdered beside the railroad tracks four miles east of Bagdad. On December 7, 1896, Louis James Searcy was arrested by T. F. Reardan, an employee of the railroad east of Danby, and turned over to Deputy J. L. Medlin at Bagdad. The evidence at the time of the arrest was the fact that Searcy was seen in the company of the victim. The story included everything traditionally found in a dime-store novel: detectives, a manhunt, intrigue, and moral justice. The spirit of Old Sleuth and the influence of dime-store novels thus cannot be underestimated as major driving forces behind the arrest and trial of the accused, Louis James Searcy. These novels and their stories of detectives working independently for the good of humanity were a blueprint for the crime, arrest, and trial described here.

Today, nothing remains of the settlements that sat adjacent to the rail lines and modern Route 66. The remnants of Bagdad are broken pieces of glass, dishes, rusting metal, concrete footings, and a lonely graveyard. If looking closely, one can find abandoned railroad ties embedded in the ground where rights-of-way once stood. Route 66 enthusiasts stop at the salt cedar tree closest to the paved road and fail to realize the true Bagdad sits to the north of the tracks. At the turn of the nineteenth century, Bagdad served as a busy support base for the Orange Blossom and the War Eagle Mine, was an important railroad service center providing helper locomotives and section houses for railroad workers, and was a vital watering stop.[13] The stories of the inhabitants are long forgotten, and nothing remains of the buildings that once stood on the vacant land. The only constant that remains is the railroad that has never stopped running through the expanse of the desert.

The information gathered for the story of Louis James Searcy came from period newspaper accounts, primary source documents from the San Bernardino County Assessor-Recorder-Clerk's office, and the California State Archives. The transcripts provided the most insight into life at these remote railroad settlements in San Bernardino County at the turn of the nineteenth century. Any derogatory terms used to describe race are not my own and are quoted directly from primary source documents.

Searcy was arrested and charged based on witness testimony, and it is difficult to determine if the witnesses' statements or actions were influenced by race. There is no question that Searcy's punishment of death was far worse than those for any of the other crimes described where suspects were identified and arrested. The story of race is complex, as there were so many nationalities and races that made up the audience and participants in San Bernardino County in 1896 to 1897, but Louis James Searcy's race definitively played a part in his arrest, conviction, and sentence of death. The conversation about race and crime and punishment in San Bernardino County at the turn of the nineteenth century begs for more research in the present day.

One thing is certain, though: the railroad created and shaped the story of the human experience and the criminal justice system in San Bernardino County in 1896 to 1897.

CHAPTER I
WELCOME TO BAGDAD

By 1892 James Albert Stewart, or J. A. Stewart, was well known by law enforcement, the San Bernardino County Board of Supervisors, and the residents of Bagdad. The self-anointed mayor of Bagdad considered his primary employment to be general merchandiser and saloon operator. The emphasis of his livelihood was always on the illegal sale of alcohol, which allowed Stewart the opportunity to partake in his favorite activity: drinking.

W. B. Broadwell, a local entrepreneur, partnered with Stewart on a joint venture and tried to legally operate a saloon at Bagdad. On July 7, 1892, the board of supervisors issued a liquor license for one year (July 1, 1892, to July 1, 1893). The partnership quickly soured, and the board of supervisors revoked the license on February 16, 1893, due to lack of payment to the county. "The license was declared revoked until said J. A. Stewart & Company shall have paid a retail liquor license for the nine months ending April 1, 1893."[14] Stewart and Broadwell parted ways, and on April 22, 1893, Broadwell placed an advertisement in the *Needles Eye*: "J. A. Stewart is no longer connected with the business at Bagdad. All persons are warned not to pay him any money, all book accounts being payable at my place of business in Bagdad."[15] In June 1894 the saloon and all its stock were lost in a mysterious fire.

Stewart's run-ins with the county continued, and in September 1894, he was arrested for assault with a deadly weapon and plead guilty to simple assault.[16] In October he was "confined to an asylum" because of "excess in drinking alcoholic stimulants," and according to the physician's report, the "patient [was] absolutely broke down in respect to his nervous system."[17] The report further described Stewart as "filthy" and "not very clean."

The midpoint between Needles and Barstow, Bagdad was the perfect place for Stewart to continue his illegal activity. On Sunday afternoon, January 26, 1896, a dozen or so Mexican contract laborers hired by the Atlantic and Pacific Railroad poured into the illegal saloon owned by Stewart. They had just been paid and wanted to drink. Stewart, a native of Missouri, was fifty-three years old and considered an old man by desert standards; standing at five-foot-eleven, he towered over the smaller-statured Mexican laborers. The saloon was the largest building at Bagdad and sat a little east, outside of the small settlement, by the water tank and coal chute. Stewart had a strained relationship with the Mexicans, who made up a majority of his customer base, as they hated him but thirsted for his services. He didn't like his customers either, or according to him, he didn't speak "Mexican." He did like the fact that they spent their money at his establishment and drank his whiskey and beer, though. It was not uncommon to hear his patrons tell him they were going to kill him! And if he caught them stealing or misbehaving, he would not hesitate to beat them with a stick. He would also use this whipping tactic to force the Mexicans to leave his bar when he was drunk and tired of serving his drunk patrons.

By nightfall, the crowd, including a twenty-eight-year-old Jesus Lopez, was belligerent and blind drunk. Once, in the past, Lopez tried to buy three bottles of beer for a dollar, but during the transaction, he tried to steal two more. Stewart caught him, and while pointing a revolver at Lopez, he ordered him to pay for his beer and demanded he never come back without his permission. On this night in particular, Stewart wanted to close the saloon and pass out because he was drunk and tired. He ordered the bar closed and demanded everyone leave the building. The crowd, now numbering ten or so, wanted to keep drinking and was angry at Stewart for closing. Stewart and his employee physically pushed the men out of the saloon; all the while, Stewart whipped them with a stick. Once outside, the crowd threw rocks, breaking the saloon windows, and someone fired a rifle into the building. Stewart then fired several shots through the saloon door, striking two of the drunks. The wounds were superficial, the crowd dispersed, and for a short time, Bagdad went to sleep. The Mexicans' hatred for Stewart grew, and they talked of burning down the saloon.

For one day, life went on peacefully, and the railroad continued its travel through the settlement. During this time, Mrs. May Rice was visiting Bagdad for three weeks and staying at the Harvey House. During her visit, she often spent time at the saloon. She understood Spanish. On one occasion, she overheard a Mexican laborer discuss how he was going to cash his $13.50 payroll check so he could buy a pistol because he wanted to shoot and kill Stewart.

On Monday Mrs. Rice spent the better part of the day in the saloon drinking port wine. Stewart, as well as his employee, John D. Henry, and a friend, John Lewis Miller, were all passing time in the saloon, and Jesus Lopez was there drinking by himself. Lopez had been drinking all day on Sunday, and after sleeping for a while, he had gotten out of bed and started drinking again on Monday. He had made his way to the saloon to drink some more when it opened, and by five o'clock in the evening, he was slobbering drunk. Stewart ordered him to leave because he didn't want a repeat of Sunday night.

Lopez initially left the saloon but, through a drunken haze, decided he wanted more to drink. He then tried to force his way in through the back door. Stewart, now angry, drunk, and armed with a revolver, pushed him out and slammed the door closed. Lopez stumbled around and fell in the yard, and once he got back on his feet, he tried to force his way back into the building through several latched doors.

Two Mexicans, Lades La Medina and Jesus Estrada, were working on top of the nearby coal chute and watched the spectacle unfold. Lopez stumbled and weaved around the building, and once he came to the side door, he was able to push his way back into the saloon. Stewart forcefully pushed him out of the building and, while doing so, pistol-whipped Lopez two or three times to the head in rapid succession. La Medina noticed Lopez had something in one of his hands, but he thought it was money to buy more whiskey.

Lopez held his head with one hand, trying to soothe the sting of the revolver strikes, but continued his momentum forward. Stewart, now enraged, raised his revolver and shot Lopez in the face from three or four feet away. The bullet entered Lopez's head one and a half inches from the outer angle of his left eye. Brain matter blew out the back of his head at the base of his skull, where the bullet left his body. Lopez was dead before his body dropped to the floor.

After the shooting, Stewart slammed the door shut and called it a night. Some of the residents of Bagdad felt pity for Lopez and covered him with a piece of canvas as it started to rain.

On January 28, 1896, Doctor A. C. Keating, the elected coroner for San Bernardino County, received a telegram notifying him there had been a shooting in Bagdad. He and Deputy District Attorney Horace C. Rolfe took the train from San Bernardino for the purposes of investigating and convening a coroner's inquest. Deputy John Lewis Medlin from Daggett was already at Bagdad waiting for the county officials. Coroner Keating impaneled a jury of seven local Bagdad residents who viewed the body and heard testimony from witnesses, four of whom were Spanish-speaking Mexican laborers who saw the shooting take place. It was a common practice for jurors and witnesses to have the opportunity to view the recently deceased and inspect the wounds and manner of death to assist in their decision-making process.

Stewart was not under arrest but testified about his own actions leading up to the shooting. Before rendering a verdict, Coroner Keating addressed the impaneled jury and gave them careful and specific directions to assist them in their decision-making process. He measured his words carefully as he spoke to the jury that sat in Stewart's saloon, the only building large enough to house the proceedings and the audience:

I want you to be careful of this proposition: There is no question how this man came to his death—the evidence shows that he came to his death by a gunshot inflicted by this man Stewart. What was the cause of the provocation, and whether he was justifiable in this matter, it is for you to say, either condemn or otherwise. I would like to say to you a little further: Understand me plainly, I am only talking to you, not instructing you—you are not to be governed by my suggestions whatever; what I say shouldn't influence you one iota. There may be something behind this. You people live here, and you know the surroundings, and you know what might happen hereafter, and if you think in your best judgement if this should go on to a preliminary examination and this thing should be thoroughly investigated, and if you think by your actions a life might be saved in the future, it is your duty to render such a verdict to see that this is done.

On January 29, 1896, the jury found that Jesus Lopez died from "a gunshot inflicted by the hand of James A. Stewart. We further find said killing was justifiable in the protection of life and property." Stewart was transported to the justice of the peace at Needles, where the case was officially adjudicated, allowing him to return to Bagdad and his illegal saloon.

Coroner Keating's warning to the jury about their decision of guilt or innocence would prove prophetic in the years to come.[18]

CHAPTER II

FRESHLY KILLED

On Sunday, December 6, 1896, at seven o'clock in the morning, Clifton Hill left his home in Bagdad, collected his tools and water, and started walking eastbound on the tracks toward Amboy. As a trackwalker employed by the Atlantic Pacific Railroad, his duties were mundane but extremely important. As he walked eastbound on the tracks, Clifton looked down and inspected the line for broken bolts, straps, and rails, which caused delays and potential derailments. Hill took his job seriously and kept steadfast track of time.

His section started a few hundred yards from the depot, and he left a little after seven o'clock in the morning, walked without a rush, and averaged two to three miles an hour. His stretch of railroad ran downhill in a straight line for seven and a half miles toward Amboy, which offered him an elevated vantage point. When he was about three miles east of Bagdad, he looked up for a moment and noticed what he thought was a man walking toward him in the middle of the tracks. He looked down again and continued to inspect the line, but when he glanced up, the figure was gone. Hill was surprised to see a man on the tracks before the section crew and figured it was just someone traveling along the line. He came across these types of travelers every two or three days and didn't think much of the lone figure.

As he reached the point where he had last seen the figure, he noticed something about thirty feet from the south side of the tracks: there was the motionless body of a male, lying on his back with his head pointed in the westbound direction. The victim's arms were at his side, and a flour sack he used as a satchel sat neatly on the ground by the body. At first, Hill thought the person was asleep, but as he looked closer from his vantage point, he could see that the person's face and beard were completely drenched in blood.

The person he had seen walking toward him from a mile away was now lying brutally murdered along the tracks. Fresh blood marked two spots where the body had been moved and then finally abandoned. The crushed creosote bushes and disturbed desert floor were evidence of a violent struggle, and there were footprints leading south, away from the body to a little knoll of an outcropping of lava. Hill looked around and came to the realization he was unarmed in the middle of nowhere at the scene of a recently committed murder—the man was freshly killed. Badly scared, he threw down his adze, wrench, and flags about one hundred feet from the body and hurriedly walked east toward Amboy to get help. He looked at his watch; it was nine o'clock. He had never seen the man before, and he had no idea why he had been beaten to death.

The first people Hill saw at Amboy were Conrad Stumpf and his men, who were putting in a rail on a sidetrack at the west switch. He checked his watch; it was 9:23 a.m. Hurriedly, he said, "I have a dead man up the track!" Stumpf seemed surprised but insisted they first replace a rail that was out. Once the repair was completed, the four-man section crew and Hill put the handcar on the track and traveled to see the body. It was close to ten o'clock when they finally left Amboy.

When they reached the body, Stumpf recognized the victim as a person he had spoken to in German an hour and a half earlier over breakfast in Amboy. Stumpf was a German immigrant from the Kingdom of Bavaria who had resided in America for fifteen years and was employed as a section foreman working in Amboy. His responsibility was the track that ran ten miles east of the settlement. He lived in Amboy with his wife, who ran the section house and made meals for the workers.

On Saturday, the day before his death, the victim walked into Amboy and knocked on Stumpf's door. He was looking ragged and asked if he could have supper, and Stumpf asked if he had money. The victim replied, "I have lots of it," and he pulled out a handful of greenbacks and coins, paid a quarter to Stumpf's wife for supper, and asked if he could sleep in the bunkhouse. Stumpf couldn't quite see how much money the victim had, but it was at least three or four dollars. Stumpf felt the victim was acting too free with his money by openly displaying it to strangers and told his wife what a foolish thing that was to do in a tough country. Leery of potential robbers, as transient section-house people were the only residents, Stumpf buried his money and valuables.

Stumpf recognized the victim's accent, and they began to speak in German. It was a nice break for the two men to converse in their native tongues, and the victim was a nice-enough man. He told Stumpf he had been working over at Franconia, in the Territory of Arizona, for two months on the section but he couldn't seem to get along with the Irishmen. Franconia was another railroad settlement located approximately one hundred miles east of Amboy. After quitting, he had traveled to Needles to pick up his discharge check and stayed for four or five days. He spent a few dollars there and then continued traveling west. He asked for a job, but Stumpf was already full handed and didn't need any men. The victim spoke of having money in the bank in San Francisco and making his way there via San Bernardino. Once he got his money, he planned on buying a good suit and then moving on to Los Angeles and Santa Barbara.

On Sunday, at 7:30 a.m., the victim ate breakfast with Stumpf and his wife while seated at their table. Before the victim left at 8:00, he lit his pipe; said he was going to try and make it to the next section house at Siberia, approximately fifteen miles west; and asked if a black man had already passed. Like many passing travelers and rail workers, the two men never learned each other's names.[19] Now, the nameless man Stumpf and his wife had enjoyed having breakfast with lay beaten to death at his feet.

The men noticed the victim was about five-foot-four or -five, fifty years old, with an average build of about 140 or 150 pounds. The blood was still fresh and caked the victim's five-inch-long beard. He wore a faded brown coat, common navy-blue working shirt, vest, and dark pants, and his old, soft brown hat was lying by his body; on his feet were brogan shoes. The victim's vest was still neatly buttoned up to the top. His sandy-reddish hair sprinkled with gray was disheveled, and it was evident the man had fought for his life. A shattered pick handle with one end covered with blood and hair lay about ten or fifteen feet from the body. There was also a large rock covered with blood and hair on the ground next to the body.

Hill reminded the men not to get off the tracks to avoid comingling their footprints with the suspect's. As Hill looked closer at the body, he noticed that the victim's legs and feet were now crossed, and he told Stumpf, "Someone has visited the body." The suspect probably knew Hill was bearing down on them and had run and hidden in the lava outcropping. From their vantage point, they had watched

Hill discovering the body and then hurriedly fled eastbound. After Hill was out of sight, the suspect must have returned to the body and tried to move it one last time.

The group of men then boarded their handcar and traveled to Bagdad to telegraph the coroner. It was now eleven o'clock.

G. W. Hess was at home in Bagdad, doing small chores and pottering around his home. It was windy and sandy, and he happened to look east toward Amboy and saw a handcar at the east switch. Wondering why it was there, he went over to the station and saw Stumpf and his trackwalker, Clifton Hill. Hess was the section foreman at Bagdad for three months before the homicide and an experienced railroad employee with eleven years of experience. He had already spent time as a section foreman in California, Kansas, Illinois, and Iowa.

Hill told him about the discovery of the homicide victim four miles east of Bagdad. As the men spoke about the discovery of the body, Hess immediately placed himself in the middle of the investigation. A fan of dime-store novels with series titles such as Old Sleuth and Ironside, Hess felt a murder committed in such a remote place would naturally make a man want to get involved. He hadn't discovered the victim's bloody body, had never met him before, and hadn't been at the crime scene. He just couldn't help himself and found a need to meddle in the investigation and take charge. Hess telegraphed the coroner in San Bernardino while the men waited outside the office. At noon, it was decided E. B. Hall, another railroad employee living at Bagdad, should be sent alone to watch the body with directions not to leave the tracks. News traveled fast in the settlement, and in a short time, approximately ten people congregated around the telegraph office and wanted to learn more about the discovery of the victim. About three hours later, the coroner directed Hess to watch the body until the deputy sheriff, John Lewis Medlin, arrived. Hess took a handcar with a small force of men, which included Clifton Hill and Walter Saunders, and traveled to the scene.

John Lewis Medlin went by J. L. Medlin and was originally from Texas but lived in Daggett, located sixty miles west of Bagdad.[20] As a constable and deputy sheriff, Medlin was the closest law-enforcement representative for San Bernardino County. He had lived in Daggett since they had built the town in 1883. His law-enforcement career dated as far back as November 1886, when he was elected as the constable of Daggett.[21] He was an experienced and respected deputy sheriff. Despite his impaired left eye and his age of thirty-eight, his energy, honesty, and dedication to duty exemplified a law-enforcement officer posted in a remote desert railroad town. He was the first official to arrive at the scene, at approximately four o'clock, eight hours or so after the discovery of the body.

When the No. 6 train stopped at Bagdad, Medlin was told a "colored man" was the suspect in the homicide. Word was spreading about a black man who had been seen in the company of the victim and was the suspect in the violent homicide. The train pulled out of Bagdad, and just as it gained speed, it slowed and allowed Medlin to jump off at the homicide scene.[22]

After a brief examination of the crime scene, Medlin helped Hess and the other men load the body onto a handcar. Medlin noticed the crime scene around the body had been trampled by the inquisitive railroad men, and he wanted to pick up the suspect's footprints leading away from the body. Medlin asked Hess if there were any tracks leading away from the body, and Hess directed him approximately seventy-five feet away from the trampled ground. At about 4:15 p.m., Medlin and Hess were the first men to follow the suspect's footprints beyond the trampled grounds. The sun was dropping, and the men, armed with revolvers, tracked the fresh prints.

The remaining men pushed and walked along the handcar carrying the lifeless body toward Bagdad. They looked back and could see Hess and Medlin looking down as they followed the tracks into the lava flow in the fading sunlight. Sand was interspersed in the lava flow, and the men could see the footprints left by the suspect. The search party grew smaller and smaller in the distance as they walked away from the railroad tracks. Medlin and Hess followed the footprints for about six miles and found them running south and west, parallel to the railroad tracks, and then into the lava beds.

Hess had a tapeline in his pocket, and they measured the footprints, which were eleven inches in length. The footprints told the story of a suspect who would run and then walk a few hundred yards at a time. Medlin was under the impression the suspect ran farthest the first time to get away from the body. The men followed the footprints for two hours, until nightfall, and then made their way back to Bagdad, reaching the settlement exhausted.

CHAPTER III
ARREST

Since September 1895, Thomas Francis Reardon, or T. F. Reardon, had been employed as the section foreman for the line of tracks running east from Danby. His work crew consisted of nameless railroad employees who came and went, typically staying for only a short time and then moving on. Reardon spent most of his life employed by the railroad and, before his arrival at Danby, worked in Colorado for ten years.[23] A thirty-five-year-old naturalized citizen and native of Ireland, he took his citizenship and oath of allegiance to the United States seriously.[24]

Located thirty-one miles east of the homicide, Danby was a smaller settlement along the Atlantic Pacific Railroad that served as a watering station for the railroad. There was a section[25] and bunkhouse, and there were several outhouses for the workers. The railroad needed these settlements—this was the only reason Danby came into existence. Originally water was piped from Bonanza Spring, approximately four and a half miles to the north, and later a well was drilled that fed a large water tank. Miners working nearby claims visited from time to time for supplies and to catch up on news from the outside world. This was T. F. Reardon's world and workday, which consisted of maintaining and repairing the nine-mile track running east of Danby. That was it, day in and day out.

Late on the evening of Sunday, December 6, freight train No. 34 pulled into Danby. Reardon always made a point to speak to the engineer because news from the outside world was always welcome. He learned a man had been found murdered east of Bagdad and didn't think much about it until one of his men reminded him of something.

"Don't you remember the man you were talking to on the handcar, the Dutchman with the whiskers?" Then it dawned on Reardon: the same man he had spoken to on Friday was the man found murdered east of Bagdad.[26]

The chatter along the railroad and between the settlements was that the suspect was the half-caste Negro who had been seen in the company of the victim with a large amount of money in his possession.

Reardon recalled what he had seen on Friday, December 4, two days before the discovery of the body. Somewhere between one and half past two o'clock in the afternoon, two men walked into Danby from the east. First a half-caste Negro, followed shortly after by an older white male who took a drink out of the water tank. Reardon approached the white male. The two men spoke for a bit, and Reardon noticed the older man had a European accent. The gentleman said he left California years ago for the "Country of Colorado," and Reardon quickly corrected him that Colorado was a state, not a country.

It seems Reardon thought a great deal of himself and was quick to correct someone in conversation. The fact that he was a citizen likely added to his self-importance. He was arrogant and belittling and always willing to brag about his accomplishments. Individuals like Reardon often thought they could have done much better in life if they were not surrounded by incompetent people.

Reardon joked, "You raised quite a crop of whiskers" as the older man had a full-grown beard. As the guest looked toward the nearby mountains, he commented that if he had the money he had spent over the last twelve months, he would prospect the hills around Danby. He went on to talk about his time working for Billy Pitts, the station foreman at Franconia in the Territory of Arizona. After earning two months of wages, he decided to leave for California because he couldn't get along with the Irish work crew at Franconia. The men spoke for about ten minutes, and he never told Reardon how much money he had made or currently had in his possession. Before arriving at Danby, he spent six days in Needles, which was filled with saloons and plenty of other establishments where a man could spend his wages.

Reardon left Danby, and when he came back from work at six o'clock, he saw the older man and the black man seated on the south side of the tracks, by the water tank. Both the men had supper at the bunkhouse and spent the night in the settlement. On the morning of December 5, a Saturday, the Negro opened the bunkhouse door and asked if he could get breakfast, and Reardon told him to ask the land-lady. Later, Reardon watched the half-caste Negro walk westbound about three-quarters of a mile and get picked up by a section gang on a handcar that was traveling west.[27]

Mrs. R. B. Weaver maintained the section and boarding house for the railroad at Danby. She was Jessie Weaver, the thirty-five-year-old wife of Rolandus Burket (R. B.), another railroad employee living at Danby. Like Reardon, she had recollections about meeting the two tramps who passed through the settlement. At about five o'clock on Friday, she was at the woodpile in the backyard when she was told a black male would like to chop wood in exchange for food. Ms. Weaver briefly spoke to the man and agreed to feed him in exchange for the labor, and when he was done, she did not see him again until Monday morning.

Mrs. Weaver also remembered feeding the older man, the victim, breakfast on Saturday morning at the boarding house. After breakfast, he asked her how much breakfast was and paid with a twenty-five-cent piece. She noticed that in the change in his cupped hand, there were silver coins and other smaller denominations. Even though this looked like a lot of money, she recalled that none of the coins were gold.[28] The men were forgotten, and Mrs. Weaver continued with her daily routine of making meals for the workers, chopping wood, and housekeeping.

On Monday, December 7, at 7:25 a.m., Reardon left Danby on a handcar heading east with his section gang of four men to start the day's work. Two of the men were Mr. Martin and Mr. Anderson, and the other two were nameless employees, as the nature of the transient labor force along the railroad meant employees came and went with little notice. As the handcar traveled along, the work crew came upon another tramp by the name of A. J. Ballard, whom they offered a ride to. It was customary for work crews to offer lone travelers rides on the handcars in exchange for the manual labor needed to propel the car forward. Even the handcar was a dangerous necessity along the railroad because the wooden parts could break, causing the person pumping the car to tumble off in front of the moving, heavy vehicle, resulting in their death. Anyone pumping the handcar had to face the direction of travel to avoid this.

Ballard pumped the handcar eastbound, and when he was two and a half miles east of Danby, the group approached a man on the railroad tracks walking eastbound. The man noticed the approaching handcar and crossed onto the south side of the tracks. As Reardon passed, he recognized the man as the same half-caste Negro who had been in the company of the murdered victim. Reardon recalled the conversation with the engineer the day before about the homicide outside of Bagdad, and in his mind, this must have been the person who committed the murder since he had seen the two men together. Without direction or advice from the authorities, he took it upon himself to act.

He ordered the handcar stopped and applied the brake, quickly arming himself with a Winchester rifle. He then stepped off the car, quickly approached the unarmed male, and pointed the rifle at him. As he did this, Reardon said, "As a citizen I have to detain you until such time turn you over to the Sheriff of San Bernardino County."[29]

The black man said not to shoot him and questioned why he was being arrested, but in his mind, it could not have been for a serious charge. Reardon told him he was going to have to take him back to Danby. At this time, the black man said his name was Louis James Searcy, or Jimmy, as he liked to be called. Reardon ordered Searcy to walk twenty feet in front of him so he could point the Winchester rifle at his back, and his work crew followed slowly along while riding on the handcar. During the walk back into Danby, he noticed that his prized homicide suspect spoke with a severe stutter.

Searcy must have asked himself if it was possible this man knew he was wanted for burglary. Searcy had recently fled Prescott in the Territory of Arizona when he was accused of burglarizing the Palace Barbershop, where he was employed for a short time.

As they reached Danby, a miner by the name of Knuckles happened to be visiting and noticed the men walking into the settlement. Mr. Knuckles had a mining claim twenty miles to the south and on occasion came into the settlement for supplies. Knuckles was a name typically assigned to men who were missing fingers, which was a common attribute in 1896.

Knuckles thought it odd the man was walking in front of Reardon at gunpoint, so he approached to watch the men slowly enter the small settlement. When Reardon saw Knuckles approach, he barked at Searcy, "Throw up your hands" and ordered Knuckles to search the unarmed man. Knuckles found $1.45, a razor, and a knife in his pockets. Knuckles was worried about the loaded rifle pointed at him during the search and nervously kept looking in Reardon's direction. During the search, Searcy flinched a little, and Reardon yelled, "Stand still, you son of a bitch." Even though Searcy was unarmed, Reardon insisted on pointing the loaded rifle at him.

Mrs. R. B. Weaver was in her kitchen when she saw the men enter the settlement and came out to watch. She recognized the black man as the person she had fed in exchange for chopping wood on Friday.[30]

Reardon relished this once-in-a-lifetime moment as it unfolded in front of Mr. Knuckles, Mrs. Weaver, and his work crew. With the audience of six, it was his opportunity to bask in the bright morning sunlight as he pointed his rifle at a homicide suspect while directing the search. Searcy was surrounded by six men and hardly in a position to attempt to run or fight, and Reardon exaggerated the situation for his own benefit. For that moment in time, Reardon was a self-anointed lawman using his citizenship as an excuse to make himself look like a hero. It was as though someone had opened a dime-store novel and painted a picture of a character acting out a scene.

For now, the situation had deescalated, and Reardon offered Searcy coffee and food, but he accepted only the coffee. Perhaps it was the fact the initial rush of self-generated adrenaline was gone; Reardon felt a need to be nice to Searcy. In his mind he had arrested a murder suspect, and the threat was gone. Mr. Knuckles got him coffee in an empty two-court tin, and Reardon asked Searcy if he wanted to go into the bunkhouse to stay warm since there was a fire going in the stove. Searcy accepted and put his feet up on a small rail surrounding the stove.

At some point, he learned he was under arrest for the murder of the white tramp, and at that moment, he realized how much trouble he was facing. His heartbeat raced, his breathing became erratic, and he could barely speak or stand up straight.[31] Searcy was under arrest for a murder committed outside of a remote settlement, and he was no longer free to leave. It was the last few moments of freedom he would have for many years.

Reardon noticed Searcy's hands and feet were shaking. "I don't know which of them kept the best time, and all the nervous disposition I ever see on a man it was him—his hand shook. In fact he had a two quart can in his hand, and his feet shook in all shape and direction, and even when he brought them to the floor then he couldn't balance himself."

After twenty minutes, Searcy asked to use the toilet house, and Reardon allowed him, as he believed "It is something you couldn't refuse a man." Reardon directed Mr. Martin, one of his crew, to shadow Searcy while he went to the water closet and stayed for approximately fifteen minutes. After he came out, he sat on the outside steps and waited for the No. 5 train to come along. Reardon went to the water closet Searcy used and, after investigating the vault area, believed it had not been used.

This arrest was the culmination of Reardon's uncelebrated life accomplishments, and he was not about to let the excitement leave his world of difficult and mundane rail work.

The three men waited about three hours for the No. 5 train, and they escorted Searcy to Bagdad, where they turned him over to Sheriff Johnnie Medlin.[32] Medlin was still at Bagdad conducting his investigation.

Medlin took custody of Searcy along with Deputy Keyes, who arrived at Bagdad at two o'clock in the morning to help assist in the murder investigation. The deputies stood by with Searcy, as they knew other officers and the coroner were on their way from San Bernardino.

Sheriff Holcomb, Deputy Arbios, and Coroner A. C. Keating traveled by train from the City of San Bernardino to Bagdad. They received word a man was found murdered between Bagdad and Amboy who was traveling with a "darkey," and it was supposed that the "darkey" had killed him.[33]

Joseph Jacob Arbios, or J. J. Arbios, was an experienced deputy sheriff and constable with twelve years of experience in San Bernardino. He was born on December 22, 1857, in the Pyrenees Mountain range between Spain and France. His family immigrated to America in 1869, when he was a small boy. He spoke five languages fluently and was, at this time, thirty-nine years old, five-foot-seven, and no stranger to this climate, as he had lived in the desert north of San Bernardino from 1876 to 1888.[34]

The train pulled into Daggett for water; there, the group was told a section boss had arrested the suspect and he was being held at Bagdad.[35] When the men arrived at Bagdad, they found Searcy in the charge of Deputy Medlin.

CHAPTER IV
CORONER'S INQUEST

In San Bernardino County in 1896, a suspected homicide, suicide, and/or accidental death fell under the jurisdiction of the county coroner. If notified of a death under these circumstances, the county coroner responded to the scene, impaneled a jury of residents, and convened a coroner's inquest to determine the cause of death. Before the inquest, the deceased would be placed on display for the jurors and the public, who were welcome to inspect the corpse and actively participate in the proceedings. The inquest was not a criminal proceeding, nor was it binding in a court of law, and the sole responsibility was to determine the cause of death. San Bernardino County newspapers routinely covered inquests and included all the gruesome and graphic details. These printed articles were published next to stories about passing circuses, advertisements, and notices of unclaimed mail. The inquest coverage allowed the reader to cross from reality to fantasy, much like a dime-store novel.

Before Doctor A. C. Keating, the San Bernardino County coroner, met Louis James Searcy at Stewart's saloon in Bagdad, he was a prominent doctor in the City of San Bernardino. He rose to power, obtained the prestigious title of physician for San Bernardino County, and was responsible for managing and treating patients at the county hospital. On January 12, 1892, Doctor Keating was appointed the superintendent of the hospital by the San Bernardino County Board of Supervisors after a recommendation by the grand jury. According to *The Daily Courier*, the move was an excellent one and guaranteed proper and honest management of the hospital. Doctor Keating was well known throughout the county, and his appointment was applauded by the community. The newspaper congratulated the San Bernardino County Board of Supervisors for their outstanding choice in the appointment.[36]

That said, his rise to prominence was short-lived, and he would again find himself in the headlines of local news, this time for all the wrong reasons. As the county physician and superintendent of the county hospital, he supervised himself. From a managerial and county-governance perspective, this did not seem to be the most prudent move, and perhaps the stress was too much for Doctor Keating.

On September 8, 1892, barely eight months after his appointment, he was seated in Department One of the Superior Court in front of the San Bernardino County Board of Supervisors. At 11:15 a.m., an administrative hearing was held; Doctor Keating was facing removal from his positions.[37] He was represented by F. B. Daley[38] and R. E. Bledsoe,[39] who took up his cause in front of the Board of Supervisors. The chairman of the board, J. N. Victor, proposed Doctor Keating be relieved of his duties as the county physician and superintendent of the county hospital. The courtroom was filled with citizens who were anxious to hear the case against him.

Mr. William V. Bidwell, a citizen and taxpayer who was interested in public affairs, filed an affidavit with the Board of Supervisors alleging Doctor Keating was under the influence of drugs while carrying out his official duties during multiple days in July 1892. On each of those days, Doctor Keating was allegedly so intoxicated that he was unfit to carry out his official duties. In this context, it is notable that throughout the nineteenth century, opium was widely prescribed in America for its ability to relieve pain. The use of drugs, specifically opium, was common, and they were legitimately obtained.

It was further alleged that on July 16, 1892, he stole seven dollars from the body of a Mr. Nobles, who died in the county hospital. During the proceedings, a nurse at the hospital, Ms. Sarah Jane Mace, testified that Doctor Keating was unsteady on his feet when he accidentally prescribed poison to his wife, who was a patient.[40] On October 4, 1892, the clerk of the board of supervisors was instructed to notify Doctor Keating that he had been removed from the office of the county physician and as superintendent of the hospital and that Doctor J. M. Hurley had been appointed. Keating was officially fired and ordered to turn all county property in his possession over to Hurley.[41]

Doctor Keating remained a practicing physician, and even though he fell from grace, he ran for public office and was elected as the county coroner in 1894. Considering the brutality of death and the size of San Bernardino County, this was not a glamorous job. Doctor Keating traveled to remote parts of the county to investigate homicides, horrific train-related accidents, and suicides.

On December 6, 1896, Doctor Keating received a telegraph in San Bernardino regarding the discovery of a homicide victim by the tracks east of Bagdad, and he gave directions to watch the body until a deputy sheriff could get to the scene. The following day, Keating left the relative comfort of San Bernardino with Sheriff Holcomb and

Deputy Arbios for the daylong trip to Bagdad. A train ride to Bagdad was far from a comfortable affair, and the men rode on benches in a dirty compartment that was rarely cleaned. A train derailment was only one of the potential threats, as passengers with transmittable diseases such as tuberculosis and typhoid rode the train and left behind microbes to be shared with everyone. It also was not uncommon for passengers to spit on the wooden floors. In sum, train travel was inherently dangerous and uncomfortable.[42] Available food on the train was nonexistent, but the group of men was lucky because there was a Harvey House lunch counter in Bagdad.

The arrival of the group of officials brought a great deal of excitement to the small settlement. Keating went about examining the body as it lay on the handcar outside the train station, noting the gruesome blunt-force trauma to the victim's face and head. He then gathered residents who were willing to participate as jurors and convened a coroner's inquest, scheduled for later in the evening. Two of the most noteworthy jurors were Clifton Hill, who discovered the victim's body, and G. W. Hess, who had tracked the suspect's footprints with Deputy J. L. Medlin. The proceedings were to take place at J. A. Stewart's saloon, and as news of the event spread, it was sure to be a packed house.

There were approximately twenty people in the building, and even though it was an official San Bernardino County proceeding, the saloon remained open, with Stewart drinking and serving alcohol at the bar. Coroner Keating officiated, and present were Searcy; Deputies Medlin, Keyes, and Arbios; and six jurors. The victim's body was moved and placed under the water tank closer to the saloon so the jurors and the witnesses had the opportunity to view it uncovered before the inquest. Searcy sat handcuffed in a corner of the saloon, and at one point before the proceedings, Deputy Keyes told him, "If I had seen you at Needles, you would have been out of this trouble." Keyes had received word Searcy was wanted for burglary in Prescott and was looking for him as he passed through Needles.

Searcy said, "No, you didn't see me, but I saw you."[43]

The audience watched, drank, and in some cases yelled their opinions, and as the alcohol flowed, they demanded Searcy should be lynched. Keating struggled to control the crowd, as Stewart was drunk and constantly interrupted and interfered with the proceedings. After asking Searcy his name, Coroner Keating stated, "I want to explain to you that it is not compulsory on you to make any statement: You can do so if you wish but if you do it is of your own free will and accord."[44] With that, Searcy understood and answered all the questions posed to him by Keating.

Louis James Searcy, "Jimmy," was born on February 5, 1858, in Kentucky. His mother lived in Los Angeles, and he spent time living and working in Washington; Texas; San Bernardino, California; and Nogales, Congress, and Phoenix in the Territory of Arizona. He was thirty-eight years old as he traveled west on foot from Needles and was referred to as a hobo or tramp. Jimmy was biracial, and on at least one occasion, his race was described as mulatto or half-caste Negro. His severe stutter made him difficult to understand, and when he was excited, he had a difficult time communicating.

Searcy was of average build and fair muscular development and suffered from ailments of the heart and lungs, which caused abnormal breathing; strenuous exercise caused his heart to beat irregularly. His chronic asthma plagued him most of his life, and his heart condition meant he was predisposed to heart disease. Any violent physical exertion, such as running or wrestling, caused him to tire quickly, and prolonged physical exertion was difficult at best.[45] The fact that he smoked exacerbated his physical condition. There were times he suffered from violent spasmodic attacks of coughing that caused him to spit up blood. This explained why he was always in good nature and was never seen in an excited manner or showing anger. He had to be reminded to slow down and speak slowly to compensate for his stutter. As he traveled along the railroad tracks, he never had more than a dollar and spare change in his pocket. Like all tramps, he was living a hand-to-mouth existence as he walked the expanse of the desert, following the rail line. The life was hard, but it was invigorating and offered freedom from the difficult life in America's cities.

While in Phoenix, he worked as a porter in a hotel and drugstore and earned a reputation as a diligent and well-liked employee. Jimmy did a little of everything, from helping guests with their luggage at the hotel to cleaning and dusting medicine bottles at the drugstore. He was entrusted with large sums of money, was good-natured, and interacted well with customers and employers. He left Phoenix for Prescott, where he worked at the Palace Barbershop for a short time until something happened and he was accused of burglarizing the establishment. According to the *Prescott Weekly Journal Miner*, he fled west the night of the burglary.[46]

The railroad was the easiest line of travel, and he knew how to survive by working for meals. The lies and half-truths that flowed from a tramp's mouth were trade commodities exchanged for a place to sleep or a meal to eat. Traveling along the railroad, the lies blended, and the strangers along the way lied in return.

Although the sites were remote, there was no shortage of tramps traveling between the section houses. They slept outside of the settlements to avoid detection, and in the morning, they continued their travel until they were exhausted, often timing a meal and a night's sleep at the following section house to "strike" the ladies selling food to the workers. In this practice, one would lie about being the victim of the Pullman Strike or a similar event to gain sympathy in exchange for food. (The Pullman Strike of 1894 was a violent conflict between employees of the Pullman Palace Car Company in Chicago and the National Guard, which was called in to quell the strike.) Such a claim was a good ploy. It was also better to approach a section house from the east to make it appear you were walking west in search of work. Once a tramp "struck" a section house, he could turn back and head the opposite direction or his original direction of travel.

A tramp could survive and travel great distances with less than a dollar in his pocket. Paying for a twenty-cent meal at one place and chopping wood or begging for one's next meal was common. Passing tramps shared information about settlements—which were fruitful and whether a given one had already been "struck."[47]

Searcy explained to the jury that he came from Prescott in the Territory of Arizona, where he lived and worked as a general house-keeper and waiter. He was headed to San Bernardino because he was familiar with the area and had worked at the Harvey House in 1889. He admitted seeing and speaking to the victim several times during his travels and meeting up with him at Danby, and he claimed the victim left Danby before he woke up and he never saw him again until he was dead at Bagdad.[48] Searcy said he met the deceased at Needles, and from there, the two traveled west and came to Blake, another remote railroad settlement west of Needles, at which time the deceased passed him. The men walked in a leapfrog manner so when one person tired, the other would pass him, and Searcy overtook the victim at Fenner as he continued to walk westbound along the tracks.

Stewart, drunk and slurring his speech, interrupted and demand-ed the right to interrogate Searcy and appear as a witness. The drunk-en audience yelled, "The son of a bitch ought to be lynched."

Medlin took notice of T. F. Reardon's comments during the in-quest: "Like a drunken man will talk if he happens to feel—that he thought he done a great deed—he arrested a wonderful murderer and so on." Reardon also yelled, "I wished that son of a bitch would have run—he would have given me a chance to fill him full of lead."[49] The saloon broke out in pandemonium, drowning out the proceedings, forcing Keating to raise his voice. J. L. Medlin stepped in with a commanding voice and calming demeanor and told the crowd no one was going to lynch Searcy and that they needed to settle down.

Searcy tried to tell the coroner's jury about some of the people he encountered during his travels while walking west toward Bagdad. On Saturday, at about three or four o'clock in the afternoon, he met another tramp, A.J. Ballard, about four miles east of Bagdad who was walking the opposite way. The two men spoke, and the tramp asked Searcy if he had stopped at Amboy and "got anything to eat." When he walked into Bagdad, he was tired, had $1.75 in his pocket, was disgusted, and was not feeling well, so he decided to turn around and head back to the Territory of Arizona. He climbed onto the roof of the Pullman car, and as it approached Danby, his hat flew off. Once the train came to a stop, he went back and found his hat and, not feeling good, stayed outside of Danby.

Searcy described walking into Danby on Monday morning about an hour before daylight and coming across the same tramp he had met outside of Bagdad. He asked the tramp if he could go buy some food from the bunkhouse, and he gave him twenty-five cents and three nickels. The tramp came back with some food, and they made coffee with some grounds the lady at the section house sold him. The coroner asked why Searcy had asked another man to get the food for him; he explained he had already asked the lady for food and did not want to strike them again. The men split a good breakfast of bread and meat and made the coffee inside of a discarded can that littered the desert.[50] At the end of his testimony the coroner's inquest was completed and the jury rendered an opinion

At four o'clock in the morning, the group of men took the train back to San Bernardino, and Arbios sat across from a handcuffed

Searcy. As soon the sun came up, Arbios noticed spots on Searcy's pants that he took to be blood, and he asked where they came from. Searcy replied, "There ain't no blood there." Arbios asked him if he had a nosebleed or if he had been in contact with anything that was bloody, and Searcy said, "No." Arbios didn't say anything else and leaned back, pulling his hat over his eyes. According to Arbios, Searcy made a cigarette, and as he watched him under the tip of his hat, Searcy began striking at the stains with his match. He told Searcy that would do him no good and he would have to rub a long while before he could rub the blood off.[51]

The case against Searcy was entirely circumstantial, and the district attorney needed to gather additional evidence to file charges. Arbios returned to the county jail with Constable John Whaley and called him down to an area where other prisoners could not hear their conversation. Arbios again asked Searcy if there was any blood on his clothes. He responded, "No, there ain't no blood on my clothes. I thought you would be putting up some kind of job on me; I ought to have someone examine those clothes before I gave them to you."

Arbios told Searcy, "I am not in the habit of putting up jobs on anyone. If you are innocent, I want to see you free as quick as anybody. All I want to do is to do what is right." He then asked again, "Have you come in contact with any animal of any kind? Have you killed any rabbits, or helped kill hogs or butcher of any kind, in order to get any blood on your clothes?"

Searcy swore he had purchased the clothes in August and no one had ever worn the clothes except him. He said he only wanted justice, and Whaley replied, "If you had justice you would have it at the end of a rope." Arbios also took Searcy's shoes, coat, vest, and pants, which he was wearing at the time of his arrest.[52] The clothing remained in the custody of the sheriff's department until it was needed at trial. Arbios paid particular attention to Searcy's shoes and noted they were well worn and one was bulging out.

On December 9, 1896, Doctor Keating completed a document titled "State of California, County of San Bernardino: Before Dr. A. C. Keating, Coroner. In the matter of the Inquisition upon the Body of _____." The deceased's name was listed as unknown, or the possible name of Joseph Falkin. The inquisition listed six jurors and described the deceased as a forty-eight-year-old native of Switzerland or Germany, weighing 150 pounds and standing five-foot-six, with gray eyes, sandy hair, and a light complexion, who came to his death on December 7, 1896. Later it was determined that the victim's true name was Joseph Otto.

"We the jury find that the deceased came to his death from injuries inflicted by a club, stone, or some blunt instrument. And furthermore, from the testimony given, we the jury conclude that there is sufficient evidence against Louis James Searcy to charge him with inflicting the injuries."[53]

On December 9, 1896, Doctor Keating logged the findings from the coroner's inquest in Coroner Logbook No. 6.[54] The inquest sealed the fate of Louis James Searcy.

CHAPTER V
EVIDENCE COMPLETE

One hundred and forty-five miles away from Bagdad, Louis James Searcy sat in the San Bernardino County Jail as the suspect in the killing of Joseph Otto. Otto, with no family or friends to claim his remains, was unceremoniously buried at the Bagdad cemetery. A neat pile of rocks outlined the grave site where he was laid to rest with the remains of others who were victims of homicide, accidents, or natural death.

The murder of Otto was a much bigger story than J. A. Stewart shooting a drunk Mexican through the back door of his illegal saloon. This was about a lone European traveler walking along the railroad tracks who was attacked, robbed, and murdered by a black tramp. There was a problem, however, with the arrest, as there wasn't enough evidence to file charges and convict Searcy. The front page of the *San Bernardino County Sun* dated December 9, 1896, barely three days after the homicide, read "The Negro Was Captured." The article described the arrest and circumstantial case and ended with "It will require more evidence that is now in the possession of the officers to convict him."[55]

Perceived justice was at a standstill, and unseen forces were trying to move the case forward. According to Arbios, physicians in San Bernardino would examine the clothing worn by Searcy, but the case still needed more evidence. The circumstantial arrest, Searcy's convoluted and hard-to-believe explanation of his whereabouts the day of the homicide, and his speech impediment didn't help his defense. He was a poor biracial tramp wearing filthy clothing, living a hand-to-mouth existence, and walking through the desert without friends or family and with only $1.45 in his pocket. He had also been seen in the company of the victim before he was murdered. He was an easy target for a homicide investigation in a far-off place whose population was mostly transient laborers who hungered for the excitement of a high-profile murder investigation and arrest.

T. F. Reardon read the newspaper and learned the filing of murder charges was doubtful. His few moments of fame were slowly fading away, and he had already bragged to anyone who would listen about the arrest. According to Reardon, Searcy was a violent homicide suspect fleeing the scene of a horrible crime. When Reardon approached Searcy, he was making for the foothills! The foothills were miles away to the south across an open desert. Searcy had nowhere to go, and Reardon was armed with a Winchester rifle, accompanied by his work crew. In Reardon's mind, this never lessened his own story of bravery. The story and the arrest were too big, and his arrogance could not let go of this once-in-a-lifetime event. Reardon had to figure out a way to provide the last bit of circumstantial evidence needed to push the case over the edge for a criminal filing. His meddling in the investigation had nothing to do with justice and everything to do with his own self-worth and the need to keep the story alive. Meanwhile, as Searcy sat in county jail, the odds were beginning to stack against him.

The spirit of Old Sleuth, the popular character from dime-store novels, spoke to Reardon and reminded him his work was not done. On December 9, two days after Searcy's arrest and three days after the murder, Reardon took it upon himself to conduct his own follow-up investigation. He went back and searched the area of the arrest and then the outhouse Searcy used the morning of his arrest. He felt so strongly about the lack of evidence and the need to keep the case alive that he directed his crew, as part of their workday, to move the wooden outhouse, which exposed the vault area containing human excrement and scrap paper. To do this, he neglected his job as a section foreman whose sole responsibility was to maintain the tracks and keep the train safely in motion.

The outhouse was divided by a shared wall, with one section for the men and the other for the women. A simple setup, with each side having a board with a hole in it above a vault where the human waste collected. Once his men removed the outhouse, he alone sorted through paper covered with fecal matter. The smell was horrible and the work was disgusting, but Reardon felt it was his duty as a citizen to continue his own personalized homicide investigation. There, at the bottom of the scrap paper, he found two ten-dollar bills. He kept searching and found a five-dollar bill even lower, at a slit in the boards leading to the lady's compartment. He called in his work gang and Ms. R. B. Weaver from the section house and laid out the money on a table for everyone to see. It was clear in Reardon's mind that he had located the money Searcy took from Otto during the commission of the robbery.

Reardon was ecstatic and took the next train to Bagdad to telegraph the coroner in San Bernardino. Based on Reardon's telegraph, District Attorney Daley and Deputy Arbios were forced to travel to Danby to gather the evidence. Arbios was not inclined to return to the desert. The last time he had seen Reardon, he was drunk at the coroner's inquest, bragging about his heroics and the arrest of Searcy. Reardon would not shut his mouth, and Arbios was not excited to hear all about the discovery of evidence. The train ride was long and uncomfortable, the weather cold, and District Attorney Daley went along, as he wanted to put the case to rest.

Reardon acted like an overstimulated child when the men arrived at Danby. The homicide case was revived, and Reardon managed to insert himself back into the investigation. One of the first things he did was to show officials the footprints left by Searcy as he walked eastbound from Danby. Arbios had Searcy's shoes with him, and he placed them on the ground by the now three-day-old footprints. The prints appeared to be generally the same size, especially the ones going eastbound from Danby. There was no doubt they were made by Searcy, and Reardon would not stop talking and pointing out the similarities. The decision was made to return to the homicide scene and follow the tracks left by the suspect. Arbios saw the scene was well trampled on and picked up the tracks once they left the disturbed area.

There was a problem. Arbios was not good at his directions and had problems deciphering which way was east or west. The points of a compass were confusing to him, and he had no formal training in how to track a human or the identification of shoe prints. He knew the train tracks ran east and west in this part of the county, but that could change quickly based on the geography of the land. Arbios followed the footprints south from the crime scene as they entered the lava fields. Walking was difficult as there were times when the ground was solid and then quickly changed to sand.

As he followed the tracks, he stopped and measured them and made a note to himself. Every so often, he would place a shoe down by the footprint and push down on it to duplicate the prints side by side. Arbios knew this was important evidence for a homicide case but figured his words would be good enough and no one would question his findings. He had testified before in criminal cases, and there had never been an issue. A seasoned and well-known deputy would not have any problems in court describing what he had seen, so he did not take the time to make a sketch or include meticulous notes to use during the trial. None of it seemed that important, nor did he want to waste any time, as the walk following the footprints was difficult. Arbios claimed he followed the footprints approximately fifteen miles through the desert and believed they made a full circle around the crater. And now Daley and Arbios felt they had enough evidence to file charges against Searcy, who sat in county jail in San Bernardino.

On December 10, the *San Bernardino County Sun* published a story: "Found Some of the Money: More Evidence Against the Bagdad Murderer. A Railroad Man finds $25 Secreted Where the Negro Had Been—Reported to the Coroner." According to the article, when Searcy was arrested and searched, the only money on his person was $1.45. Reardon telegrammed the coroner, stating, "Have found $25 in the toilet house here but am not through searching. Two ten-dollar bills and one five."

The spirit of Old Sleuth was alive and well, and Reardon was once again in the headlines. The article also read, "little by little it seems if the coils were being tightened around the negro who is now in jail, and who the officers believe is guilty of the crime."[56] Reardon was the person tightening the coils. Reardon, with the help of Arbios, pushed the case over the edge; there was nothing stopping the wheels of justice now.

On December 11, F. B. Daley sent the following telegraph to San Bernardino to L. M. Sprecher,[57] assistant district attorney: "Have Grand Jury meet next Wednesday to hear negro case. Will subpoena witnesses for that day. Evidence complete. F. B. Daley."

The same day, a telegraph was received in San Bernardino addressed to Sheriff Holcomb: "Prescott, Arizona, December 11, 1896. Dear Sir, your telegram with description of Searcy received. He is the same man that I have a warrant for burglary. Please let me know the result of his examination on the charge of murder which you have against him. If it should be that you can't hold him on that charge wire me and I will come and get him. Very respectfully C. G. Ruffner."[58]

The arrest and the investigation of the murder were like a dime-store novel read aloud, and Reardon was the author.

CHAPTER VI
THE ATTORNEYS

Willougby Rodman wrote in the *History of the Bench and Bar of Southern California* (1909):

> The Evolution from the ancient Mexican laws under which the people of California lived, to the system that now prevails, has been rapid and emphatic. But few years have elapsed since California was part of Mexico; then followed the days of Western Frontier law and justice, unwritten on the books, but none the less understood and accepted; now the civilized code and its ethics. During the transition period, men of mighty brain have distinguished the California bar, and added to the fame a fair state. It is of these legal giants and their work that much of this review will treat men of steadfast purpose and hardy courage, whose precept and example will ever serve as inspiration for succeeding generations.[59]

The perfect storm of recent law school graduates and the want of legal defense experience created Searcy's defense team. Three attorneys, none of whom were over the age of twenty-seven, took up the cause and worked tirelessly. Deputy Arbios had no idea the defense and ensuing trial would be such a topic of discussion in the newspaper and for the population of San Bernardino.

THE DEFENSE

60

Benjamin Franklin Bledsoe, or B. F. Bledsoe, was born and raised in San Bernardino and was the most outspoken of the three attorneys, taking the leadership role in the defense team. He was born on February 8, 1874, attended local schools, and graduated San Bernardino High School in 1891. He then attended Leland Stanford Junior University and was admitted to the bar on October 3, 1896. He joined his father's law firm, which became Bledsoe and Bledsoe, located on the Bogart Block in San Bernardino. His father, R. E. Bledsoe, represented Doctor A. C. Keating in 1892 when the board of supervisors heard the case against him for being under the influence of drugs or alcohol while serving as the county physician and superintendent. His father also served as the district attorney for San Bernardino County in 1883. B. F. Bledsoe had been an attorney for two months and was twenty-three years old when he took on the defense of Louis James Searcy in a capital murder case.

61

Henry Montague Willis, or H. M. Willis, was born November 12, 1871, in San Bernardino. He was one of twelve children, though only seven of the children attained years of maturity. His ancestors were among the first English settlers of the colony of Virginia. H. M. Willis was the third namesake and a second-generation attorney. His father came to San Bernardino in 1858 to practice law and became an expert in land titles and water rights. His legal record was marked by impartiality and by a clear and decisive appreciation of justice and equity. These traits were passed on to his son.[62] In 1886, his father was a judge for a term of two years until retiring from the bench, and he remained active in law practice as the senior partner of the firm of Willis and Cole.[63]

H. M. Willis Jr. graduated from the University of California and was admitted to practice in 1894. He was the senior defense attorney, with two years of legal experience under his belt.[64] He received his early education at the Mission District School of Old San Bernardino and at Sturges Academy. He graduated from the University of California with a PhB (bachelor's of philosophy), and he attended Hastings College for one term before he was admitted to the bar in San Francisco on January 9, 1894. He practiced in San Bernardino and Phoenix beginning in 1895 as a member of Cox and Willis and Flannagan and Willis. He had just turned twenty-six years old at the time of the trial.[65]

Gordan Hall was born in Piqua, Ohio, on December 18, 1870, and his early education was obtained in both Ann Arbor and Marquette, Michigan. He went to college at Trinity in Harford, Connecticut, and graduated in 1892; after graduation, he went to Harvard Law School. Shortly following completion of his law degree, he became a junior member of Otis, Gregg, and Hall of San Bernardino. He was twenty-seven years old, and at the time of the trial, he was the eldest of the three defense attorneys.[66] As the least experienced of the three, he played a lesser role in the defense and trial.

These three attorneys were intelligent and respected men of the community, and Bledsoe and Willis would have absolutely known each other, as they were both born and raised in San Bernardino. They were also born before the arrival of the railroad in their part of San Bernardino County. Coincidentally, Willis met Searcy while working in Phoenix and was the most emotionally vested in the case. He stayed at the hotel where Searcy worked and knew of his good nature and laid-back personality firsthand. The group of three defense attorneys made a formidable team, but their immaturity and lack of experience harmed them, and they came across as arrogant and condescending.

THE PROSECUTION

District Attorney Frank Barber Daley was born on May 13, 1861, in San Bernardino County and was the son of Edward and Nancy Hunt Daley. He received his education in the public schools of San Bernardino and Oakland High School and was admitted to the bar by the Supreme Court of Los Angeles in 1887. He practiced in San Bernardino and was the district attorney of San Bernardino County from 1895 to 1899.[67] He was thirty-five years old at the time of the trial.

Deputy District Attorney Luther Melanchthon (L. M.) Sprecher was born on March 9, 1849, the son of Samuel and Catherine (Schmucker) Sprecher. He graduated from Wittenberg University in Springfield, Ohio, in June 1870 and studied law with S. A. Bowen in Springfield. He was admitted to the bar in Cincinnati, Ohio, in 1873. He moved to California in March 1883 and was admitted by the Supreme Court of California in 1888 while engaged in practice in San Bernardino.[68] He was forty-seven years old when he assisted in the prosecution, playing a minor role in the trial.

THE JUDGE

Frank Frederick Oster was born on June 3, 1860, in Sparta, Wisconsin, the son of M. P. and Magdalena Oster. He was married on October 15, 1891, to Elsie Donald and received his education in public schools in Sparta. He graduated from the University of Wisconsin in 1882 and was admitted to the bar in Wisconsin in 1885, moving to California in 1886. He opened a law office in Colton in 1887, then started on organization of the City of Colton in 1888, where he was elected city clerk and appointed city attorney, a post he held for four years. He was elected to be the district attorney of San Bernadino County and the judge of the Superior Court in 1893.[69] At the time of the trial, he was thirty-seven years old.

CHAPTER VII

PRETRIAL

In preparation for the trial, Bledsoe filed a motion for continuance, laying out the strategy of the case. He recognized the case was circumstantial and that Searcy's best defense was an alibi, and he argued his client was twenty-five miles east of the crime scene outside of Danby. Because of this, he needed to locate witnesses to support his argument. The motion described Searcy as a "total stranger" to the area who encountered individuals he would recognize by sight only and would not know their names. The witnesses would have to be located by a competent person who would travel to the area, 160 to 190 miles from San Bernardino. Some of the potential witnesses were railroad workers assigned to specific trains that passed at certain times. Finding them would require the study of train reports at Barstow and other stations along the Atlantic and Pacific Railroad.

Bledsoe's motion depicts Searcy as being in absolute poverty and unable to hire anyone to search for possible witnesses. Bledsoe thus secured the services of E. F. Pourade, a private investigator who could and would, in two weeks, be in the desert, attempting to locate said witnesses. Bledsoe went on to argue that because Searcy had another attorney for a short time, he was further delayed in preparing for the trial. Later in the same motion, Bledsoe wrote, "Affiant (Searcy) states that he is and has been from youth afflicted with an impediment of speech which has made it very difficult and required a great deal of time to put his counsel in possession of the facts of his defense. That therefore affiant has not had sufficient time since the appointment of his said counsel to prepare for his defense."[70]

Bledsoe wrote to Searcy's former employers asking for letters describing his demeanor when he was working for them; he also solicited funds for his defense. On January 18, 1897, a former employer, N. V. Walsh, described Searcy as a law-abiding employee who worked for him as a porter at the Sixth Avenue Hotel in Phoenix, in the Territory of Arizona, for almost a year. He described Searcy as a "good industrious law-abiding citizen to the fullest extent. I am sure he would be spoken of as the best by all who were in our hotel during his service." Mr. Walsh added, "It would grieve us most deeply to hear he was unjustly punished, and we all believe his innocence of this crime." He ended the letter by asking Bledsoe to keep him apprised of the trial.

Mr. Edward Butt, president of the Phoenix Drug Company, also wrote a letter on behalf of Searcy, who was employed as a porter and janitor for ten months. Mr. Butt stated, in part, that Searcy "was a thoroughly honest and a law-abiding citizen."

Another request for continuance describes the location of the crime as "rough, wild, almost wholly uninhabited except by some few mining prospectors and by certain employees of the Atlantic and Pacific Railroad who are continually moving from place to place

In the Superior Court

OF THE

COUNTY OF SAN BERNARDINO, STATE OF CALIFORNIA.

The People of the State of California .... Plaintiff.

vs.

Department One.

Louis James Shorey .... Defendant.

The People of the State of California send Greeting to

John Medlin and John Doe Nuckles, Danby.

We Command You, *That all and singular business and excuses being laid aside, you appear and attend*

before **Department One** *of our Superior Court of the County of San Bernardino, State of California, at a term of said Court to be held at the Court House in said County on* Tues *day, the* 7 l" *day of* February *A.D. 189* 7 *at* 1 0 *o'clock* 9 *M., then and there to testify in the above stated cause, now pending in the said Superior Court, on the part of* defendant

and for a failure to attend you will be deemed guilty of a contempt of Court and liable to pay all loss and damages sustained thereby to the party aggrieved, and forfeit one hundred dollars in addition thereto.

FRANK F. OSTER

Witness, *HON. GEO. E. OTIS, Judge of the said Superior Court, at the Court House in the County of San Bernardino, this* 20 *day of* February *189* 7

Attest, *My hand and seal of said Court the day and year last above written.*

Jr. U. J. Dии .... Clerk.

By J. S. Wood

Deputy Clerk.

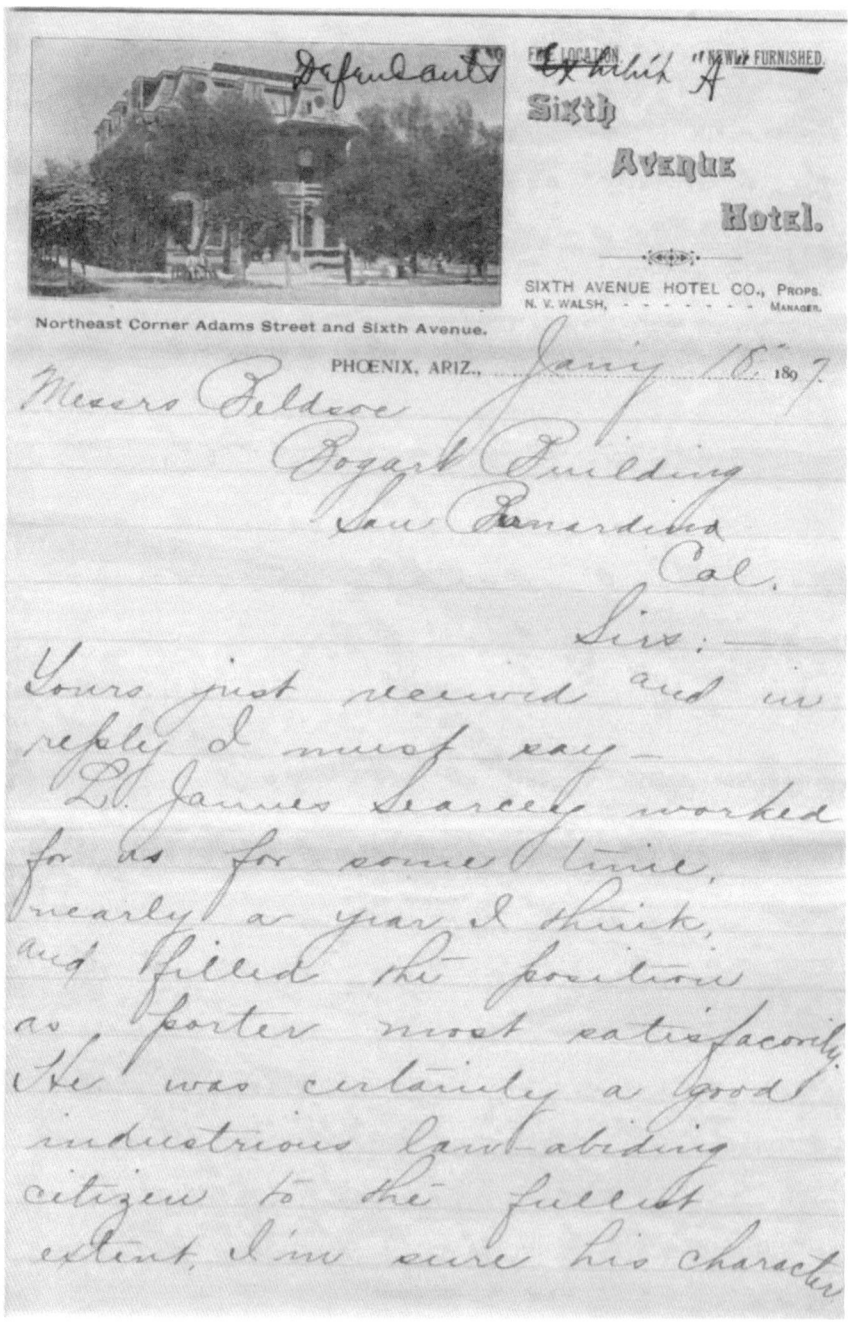

Northeast Corner Adams Street and Sixth Avenue.

Defendant's Exhibit "A"

NO FINE LOCATION "NEWLY" FURNISHED.

Sixth Avenue Hotel.

SIXTH AVENUE HOTEL CO., PROPS.
N. V. WALSH, - - - - - - - MANAGER.

PHŒNIX, ARIZ., *Jany 18th* 189 7

Messrs Beldsoe
Bogart Building
San Bernardino
Cal.
Sirs:—
Yours just received and in
reply I must say—
Lt James scarcely worked
for us for some time,
nearly a year I think,
and filled the position
as porter most satisfactorily.
He was certainly a good
industrious law abiding
citizen to the fullest
extent, I'm sure his character

72

along the line of said railroad." And due to the distance from San Bernardino, the defense was forced to rely on letter-writing to gather evidence. The defense was also waiting to hear back from cocounsel Henry M. Willis, who interviewed and deposed potential witnesses in Phoenix.[73]

On February 18, H. M. Willis interviewed W. Howe, Charles F. Morgan, Ed Butt Jr., Frank Pierce, and N. V. Walsh. He asked all the potential witnesses a series of questions about Searcy. The witnesses knew Searcy from his employment at the Sixth Avenue Hotel, where he worked as a porter from spring until November of 1896.

The responses included a description of Searcy. One wrote, "I know they (employers and guests) all spoke very highly of Jimmie." Another explained, "I know Jimmie was frequently trusted with sums of money and he regularly carried money from the Hotel to our store in the sum all the way from five to $60.00. I also know that the people and guests about the Hotel always considered Jimmie reliable and thoroughly honest during the time I boarded there."

Finally, H. M. Willis attested, "I saw him almost every day about the hotel for six or seven months and I never saw him raise any disturbances, but on the contrary was very quiet and a mighty good-hearted boy."[74] Willis also knew him as a porter at the Phoenix Drug Company and the Morgan and Howe's grocery store.

CHAPTER VIII

THE TRIAL
FEBRUARY 23–MARCH 4, 1897

A t ten o'clock in the morning on February 23, 1897, a little over two months after the arrest of Louis James Searcy, the jury men were called to Department One of the Superior Court of the County of San Bernardino. Present in the court room were the Honorable Judge Frank Oster, Sheriff G. L Holcomb, and Deputy Clerk L. A. Pfeiffer. That day the defendant was present and represented by his counsel, B. F. Bledsoe and Gordan Hall, and the people were represented by District Attorney F. B. Daley. The shorthand reporter was ordered to take down the testimony of the proceedings. The defense attorneys were well spoken, but their mastery of the English language was unintentionally arrogant and condescending. As much as Bledsoe and Willis, who would later join the defense, were from San Bernardino, they stood apart from the jurors.

Bledsoe challenged the entire panel and argued potential jurors who were in possession of their natural faculties were not called because the county had not updated the last assessment role. This was a valid argument since there were no potential names of jurors from the Township of Colton. Potential jurors came from Ontario, Redlands, Cucamonga, Del Rosa, Rialto, Cajon, Mission, Central, Highland, Daggett, and the City of San Bernardino. The jurors were like the witnesses and deputy sheriffs—transplants from throughout the United States and immigrants from Europe. And unlike the defense attorneys, they were farmers, miners, and vintners who traveled great distances to the city and lost money because they were taken away from their respective livelihoods. On the other hand, the defense attorneys were well dressed, and their conversation was hard to track because they spoke in an exaggerated Victorian manner.

Bledsoe made a motion that H. M. Willis be entered as associate counsel for the defendant, which was granted. There were now three defense attorneys representing Searcy. Further defense motions were denied by the judge before the case began.

PROSECUTION OPENING STATEMENTS

District Attorney F. B. Daley started the trial with an articulate and captivating opening statement that overtook nineteen pages of court transcript. Daley admitted the case was entirely circumstantial and argued suggestions made during the trial *should be considered fact.* The evidence was foolproof! Witnesses would testify about the discovery of the victim's body four miles east of Bagdad in the Great Mojave Desert. The victim's face and head were all mashed, bruised, and bleeding, and the weapons lay by the body. A five-cent piece was found by the victim's side, and there was an indication the victim was searched, as his pocket had been turned inside out.

"The country where the body was found are lava beds where years ago there was a violent volcanic eruption. And gentlemen, where that man was murdered, or rather he was found, was about midway between the railroad track and the point where those lava beds come nearest to the track. The body was within one hundred feet of the tracks, indicating that the *person or persons, if such be the case*, dragged that body from where it was killed or attempted to drag it to those lava beds" (italics added).

This was the first and only time the prosecution would admit it was possible there were two suspects involved in the homicide. The prints indicate the suspect left and then returned to the body from the outcrop of lava. That outcrop was elevated and offered concealment with a clear and unobstructed view of Amboy, which was at a lower elevation. Anyone walking westbound on foot from Amboy could be seen by the naked eye from this vantage point. The prints of the suspect led eastbound, parallel to the tracks, and then southeast around the volcano, where they disappeared. While retracing the suspect's path, Arbios took Searcy's shoes with him and placed them into the tracks; it was a seemingly perfect fit. The shoes also had a peculiar imprint caused by the worn-out soles, and the sides or uppers were busted out. The deputy took the shoes with him for ten or fifteen miles. According to Daley, the shoe prints were identical to the ones worn by the suspect. So the footprints were an important part of the prosecution.

THE TIMELINE

Friday, December 4, 1896

Witnesses place Searcy and the victim together at Danby, where they both spent the night at the settlement. Unlike the victim, Searcy chopped firewood for his meal. In the morning, the two men began walking westbound, with Searcy leaving first, followed by the victim. There was no question the suspect and the victim were in close proximity and had encountered each other since leaving the Needles.

Saturday, December 5, 1896

Searcy arrived at Amboy at about two o'clock in the afternoon, only to stop and fill his glass water bottles before he continued to walk westbound toward Bagdad. While walking toward Bagdad, he met another tramp or hobo by the name of A. J. Ballard, who was walking eastbound in the opposite direction. The men briefly spoke, and the tramp asked Searcy if he could "strike"[75] the lady at the section house at Amboy. Searcy replied that the section foreman had already shared some food with him and he seemed all right. The two men then parted ways.

The victim arrived at Amboy at about six o'clock in the evening, long after Searcy's departure. Exhausted and having money for food, the victim stayed the night at Amboy. Ballard, having passed Searcy several hours earlier, also arrived at Amboy and spent the night. In the morning, Ballard left Amboy, walking eastbound, and arrived at Danby on Sunday night, where he spent the night.

Sunday, December 6, 1896

Again having money to spend, the victim ate breakfast at 7:30 a.m. and left Amboy, walking westbound along the tracks toward Bagdad. The victim was murdered at approximately nine o'clock in the morning and was discovered by Clifton Hill, a trackwalker, four miles east of Bagdad. The victim was freshly killed, and the creosote bushes and dirt surrounding his body were torn up and disturbed, indicating the victim fought for his life.

Monday, December 7, 1896

In the early hours of Monday morning, Searcy awakened Ballard, who was unaware of the homicide as he slept on a stack of railroad ties outside the settlement of Danby. Searcy offered to buy food for them both if Ballard would get up, put on his shoes, and buy the grub from the woman at the section house. Ballard asked why he didn't buy breakfast himself, and Searcy said, "I *worked* the old lady on Friday, and she made me cut wood for the food, and I don't want the lady to know I had money all along."[76]

Because of Searcy's stutter, Ballard was having a hard time understanding him. Ballard asked where he got money, and Searcy lied and said he had been paid a dollar for some work in the kitchen at the Harvey House at Bagdad. He then gave Ballard forty cents to buy a twenty-five-cent meal and some smoking tobacco and cigarette paper. It was still dark when Ballard approached the section house, and he was asked to come inside to have breakfast, but he declined, saying there were two of them. He bought some meat and bread for twenty-five cents and some Durham tobacco and rolling paper for ten cents and gave Searcy back the nickel change.

The two men went outside, ate their breakfast, and talked about traveling east. Searcy left first, and Ballard thought about staying the night at Danby, but he changed his mind and started walking eastbound as well. After walking for a short time, he was picked up by a work crew traveling along the tracks on a handcar. The handcar traveled a few miles before passing Searcy, and Reardon recognized him as the same person who had been in the company of the victim and ordered the handcar stopped. He then pointed a rifle at Searcy and ordered him to stop.

Reardon walked Searcy back to Danby at gunpoint. It was there they waited for the next westbound train to take them to Bagdad, where there was a telegraph office. While they waited, Searcy was searched for weapons and was found in possession of a broken white-handled razor and an ordinary pocketknife. While waiting for the train, Searcy asked to use the water closet, where he stayed for about fifteen minutes, his coat and vest hanging outside.

After arriving at Bagdad, Searcy was searched again in detail by law enforcement and found to be in possession of $1.45. He was interrogated by the officers and was asked where he got the money, and he said, "I had $1.75 when I left Arizona and brought it with me, and down at Danby on Monday morning, I struck a hobo, and he had fifteen cents, and I had twenty cents, and we put it all together, and he went up and brought some grub and some tobacco for it." Daley argued there was a discrepancy in Searcy's claim about giving Ballard money to buy food.

Tuesday, December 9, 1896

The officers asked the defendant, "What made you turn back when you were going west to California?" Searcy said he had already worked in California at the Harvey House in San Bernardino and had not liked it. He changed his mind and headed back east, deciding to return to the Territory of Arizona.

On Tuesday, Reardon learned the Negro had $1.55 and went into the water closet and overturned it. There, rolled up in a little wad of greenbacks, shoved down underneath the water closest, among the offal, was twenty-five dollars in currency. Further, there was no indication the water closet had been used when the colored man had been in there. "We will establish by testimony that the defendant was on his way from the Territory of Arizona, evading officers."

CLOSING

Daley made much of the fact that Searcy reached Bagdad but changed his mind and turned back and was walking back eastbound past Danby. He did so even though he knew he was wanted for burglary in Prescott and would be traveling toward awaiting officers. He also pointed out Searcy had a razor in his possession, which was stolen during the burglary in Prescott.

Daley repeatedly told the jury about the blood on Searcy's clothes, which Searcy denied being present. During the opening statement, Daley mockingly imitated Searcy by saying, "'No blood on my pants.' Oh, pshaw, that is blood on your pants."

When Searcy was put into the county jail, two officers were in there talking to him. They said to him, "How did you get that blood on there?"

He replied, "There never was any blood!"

"Didn't your nose bleed, or didn't you kill a rabbit or something?"

"No, sir, there was never any blood on there."

"Where did you get those clothes?"

"I bought them in a store there."

"What store?"

"It was in Arizona."

"Have you worn those clothes all the time since you bought them?"

"Yes, sir."

"No one else ever had them on?"

"No, sir."

Reputable physicians from San Bernardino who would later testify the clothing worn by Searcy was covered with blood.

Then there was the matter of a motive for the killing. Otto, the victim, was an ordinary section hand on the railroad at or near the station of Franconia on the border of the Territory of Arizona. On or about November 24, he quit work, going to Needles. He obtained two paychecks from the railroad, for the twenty-fifth and twenty-seventh of the month, in the amount of thirty or thirty-three dollars. Since Searcy traveled with the victim, he knew he was in possession of a large amount of money. Daley argued:

> That at Danby and before they reached there this defendant knew the old man had money. That he knew that the old man bought his provisions; that the old man was one of these men—there are a great many in the world—who do a great deal of talking about what they have. He was a talkative man and told everybody what he had; and when they came on the old man showed the money wherever he was and the negro knew it. And there, gentlemen, we will attempt to establish the motive in this manner: that when the old gentleman was found no money was found on his person. One solitary nickel was found by his side as if dropped in haste. We will establish by evidence that this defendant never was on Sunday or for months prior to in the station at Bagdad that Sunday or at any time. Remember, that we are to prove that he was not at Bagdad on that day; that he did not work at the Harvey House and that they did not pay him a dollar or any other sum—not a nickel.

The implication was that Searcy had traveled with the victim since Needles and knew he was in possession of a large amount of money. He then traveled in front of the victim after arriving at Amboy. He then waited for the victim to leave Amboy and surprised him and robbed him before he reached Bagdad. During the robbery, he killed the victim by striking him in the face and head with a rock and a pickax handle. Daley concluded:

> That is the line of testimony that we propose to establish, and I have tried to outline to you as best I could. There are a great many circumstances connected with it and it is difficult to keep them all in your mind. But I want you to try and do it; and as we present the witnesses before you, I wish you to remember each of these separate facts as I have outlined them so that you can readily apply the testimony to them and understand the places and different locations. And with that I will now leave you to listen to the testimony.[77]

CHAPTER IX
THE TESTIMONY

Thirty witnesses testified during the ten-day trial, which generated 541 pages of neatly typed transcript. Except for a handful, most witnesses were called by the prosecution to prove the circumstantial case. Their testimony offers a window into life along the railroad settlements dotting the uninhabited Mojave Desert in 1896. A few were unwitting participants, while others inserted themselves into a highly publicized homicide. The discovery of a dead body four miles east of Bagdad was an adventure unfolding in a remote part of the American West and begged for public participation and attention.

G. W. Hess and Clifton Hill were two of six jurors the night of the drunken coroner's inquest, with Hess acting as the foreman. That cold December night at Bagdad, they heard the demands for a lynching and a drunk T. F. Reardon bragging about the arrest and saying he wished Searcy had run so he could have shot him. Coroner A. C. Keating recorded the coroner's jury findings, which found Joseph Otto most likely died at the hands of Louis James Searcy. The witnesses could never turn back or waver from their version of events as presented at the coroner's inquest.

Hess testified again at the grand jury, along with T. F. Reardon, A. J. Ballard, J. J. Arbios, and Doctor McKechnie. These five men, especially Reardon, were pivotal in the arrest, indictment, and subsequent trial. As witnesses for the prosecution, their testimony was the case against Searcy. The prosecution built the entire case around their testimony, and the remaining witnesses were only called to support their version of events.

Two witnesses subpoenaed by the prosecution, Doctor G. A. Rene and Deputy J. L. Medlin, stood firm in their beliefs and refused to support the evidence presented by the prosecution. In a slow and deliberate manner, Deputy J. L. Medlin disagreed with other witnesses about the shape of the footprints. He was the deputy who initially conducted a crime scene investigation and was not called to testify at the coroner's inquest or the grand jury. Doctor Rene questioned the expertise and the ability of the other physicians who claimed blood corpuscles were present on the pants belonging to Searcy. He stated the identification of blood corpuscles was an imperfect science and should not be used as evidence in sentencing a man to death. Indeed, every single witness and juror understood a guilty verdict meant Louis James Searcy would die at the end of a rope at San Quentin State Prison.

Searcy was the last to testify during the trial, doing so in his own defense. It was his burden to explain away the preceding twenty-nine witnesses.

Judge Oster sympathized with Searcy and told him to speak slowly and clearly so the jury could understand him through his stutter. The jury listened intently, as this was the first time they had heard him speak aloud. Searcy admitted he met the victim on Thursday, December 3, 1896, eleven miles east of Needles, as they traveled westbound on foot along the railroad. He explained that he saw the victim intermittently as the men walked at different speeds and leap-frogged each other.

Searcy encountered him again on the afternoon of Friday, December 4, 1896, at Danby, when the victim walked into the settlement. Searcy had arrived several hours earlier and had already chopped fire-wood for a meal. The two men spoke to each other and spent the night in the bunkhouse. Searcy claimed the next time he saw the victim, he was dead at Bagdad, lying under the water tower, covered with a blanket.

On Saturday, December 5, 1896, the morning after Searcy and Otto spent the night in the Danby bunkhouse, Searcy had left the bunkhouse at 6:45 a.m. and started walking westbound when a work crew picked him up and gave him a ride on their handcar. He traveled with them for about seven or eight miles until they let him off, and he continued walking until around noon, when he arrived at another section house twelve miles east of Danby. He couldn't remember the name of the settlement, but it was most likely Cadiz. There, he chopped kindling wood in exchange for lunch, eating half and saving the other half in his pocket. After spending twenty-five to thirty minutes in the settlement, he continued walking west until he encountered a work crew and a train that passed going westbound.

His next stop was a sidetrack, where he met a trackwalker who was sitting down, with his shoes off, eating lunch. The trackwalker gave him some beans, a big piece of cake, and two slices of bread with meat and butter. He ate the beans, and he shoved the rest of the food into his pocket for later. After talking for a while, the two men walked west, and Searcy continued when the trackwalker stopped to do some work. Searcy then stopped at Amboy at about three or four o'clock, where he watched workers picking up scrap iron, filled up his beer bottle with water, and continued to walk westbound.

About a mile and a half from Amboy, Searcy met A. J. Ballard, another tramp, who was traveling eastbound. Ballard told Searcy he was a "damned fool" for going west as there was no work. He also warned Searcy not to expect to get any food at Bagdad as the settlement was filled with Mexicans.[78] It was then about four o'clock in the afternoon, and the two tramps spoke for about twenty minutes. The totality of the conversation is lost to time, but one would have to think the men discussed law enforcement because they were both hobos and trying to avoid being arrested for vagrancy. The railroad did not take kindly to tramps and wanted to rid them from passing trains.

Searcy slowly continued walking westbound; all the while, three or four trains passed him going eastbound, and he commenced having a bad headache. When he arrived at Bagdad, he stopped about one hundred yards from the settlement and sat down and smoked. He also ate some of the food he had saved in his pocket. It was a little after dark now, and he thought about his next move, deciding to turn back eastbound. He didn't speak to anyone, nor did he make a point of being seen.

Searcy eventually found himself lying along the tracks, resting by the coal chute until he heard the train coming. The engine pulled under the water tank to take water, and once the whistle blew, he put his jacket on, turned up his collar, and climbed onto the Pullman car, which was always the last car on the train. He stepped on the brake wheel and pulled himself onto the roof. He then crawled on his hands and knees and lay flat until the train pulled out of the settlement. According to Searcy, he picked his head up and his hat blew off about five miles west of Danby. Crossing the open desert, he knew he needed his hat, so he counted the trestles as the train passed over them to measure how far back his hat was. At about nine o'clock at night, the train pulled into Danby, and Searcy walked back. After a long search, he found his hat about one hundred yards from the tracks. He then started walking east, back toward Danby, and after about a mile, he stopped and made a fire to keep warm.

It was now Sunday, December 6, between one and two o'clock in the morning. Searcy, not feeling well, lay down and fell asleep beside the tracks until a little bit before eight o'clock, when a track-walker passed him. Joseph Otto was about to be murdered four miles east of Bagdad and approximately thirty-one miles away from Danby. This was an approximately eleven-hour nonstop hike by foot walking along the tracks.

Drowsy, Searcy went back to sleep; a passing train woke him up at about eleven. He still wasn't feeling well and fell back to sleep, then woke up when it was getting dark and built a fire to stay warm. After about two hours, he started walking toward Danby, hoping to catch the same train he caught on Saturday. To his misfortune, the train passed him before he arrived at the settlement. He stopped and built another fire to keep warm and slept a few hours, and then he woke up. Searcy made a point of staying outside of the settlement.

It was now Monday, December 7, sometime before sunrise. At about seven o'clock, he saw another fire blazing about thirty feet from the tracks. He decided to walk to the fire and found A. J. Ballard sleeping with his coat and vest under his head and his back to the fire. Ballard also made a point to sleep outside the settlement. Searcy said, "Hello there, Bo."

Ballard jumped up and said, "Don't I know you?"

Searcy told him, "Let's go up under the bunkhouse and get out of the wind."

As they started walking toward Danby, Ballard said he had not had anything to eat since Saturday. Searcy offered to chip in money, giving Ballard forty cents, and told him to buy some smoking tobacco as well. Ballard returned with food, coffee grounds, and tobacco.

After eating their breakfast, Searcy left Danby heading east, while Ballard stayed in the settlement for a bit. Shortly after, he would be arrested by Reardon at the point of a Winchester rifle.

Searcy testified the stains and spots on his pants were from sleeping in boxcars and riding on brake beams under trains. His pants were covered with filth and stains, and it would have been hard to discern bloodstains from filth. He had purchased the pants in October and had been wearing them nonstop without a change of clothing. There were also stains from liquid spilling from drug bottles when he worked in a drugstore in Phoenix. He further testified he had had nosebleeds since owning the pants and had coughed up blood, so if there were any bloodstains, they would have come from those instances. The argument by the prosecution that blood was present on his pants was a major strength in the case.

During the last part of cross-examination by the prosecution, Searcy claimed it was Deputy Medlin who first asked if he had any blood on his clothing. And during the coroner's inquest, Medlin and Deputy Keyes took him outside of the saloon and closely examined his clothes. They looked at his shoes and stockings, unbuttoned his vest, and looked at his undershirt and pants. Keyes examined his hat, and neither of the deputies found any spots of blood. He had $1.90 on December 6 and kept it in his watch pocket and in his shoe to hide it from the brakemen.

Clifton Hill, the trackwalker who discovered the murder victim, was the first to testify. Hill looked and spoke like the jurors, and because of that, the men of the jury liked him. His soft-spoken and articulate way of testifying was believable, and he would be the only witness to admit he was frightened when he discovered the lifeless body. His lack of bravado or self-importance weighed heavily on the jury's decision. As a railroad employee, Clifton Hill followed the rules and left for work on time as for all good railroad employees, time was important. He looked at his watch and noted the time when he discovered the body and when he reached Amboy looking for help. He was the first to testify about discovering footprints at the scene of the crime—the footprints in the lava-strewn desert leading away from the body were an integral part of the prosecution's case. Hill testified he first thought the tracks were made by pointed-toed shoes but then, two days later, he changed his mind and believed the prints were made by square-toed shoes. He admitted seeing Searcy wearing square-toed shoes at the coroner's inquest. His change in testimony assisted the prosecution.

During Hill's examination by the prosecution, he described the buildings at Bagdad but forgot to include several of them in his testimony. This lack of clarity sparked a sharp and nasty rebuke from twenty-seven-year-old Harvard-educated Gordan Hall, who was the least experienced of the defense attorneys. The jury would remember this perceived mistreatment of a witness.

As soon as G. W. Hess, the section foreman at Bagdad, heard of the crime, he could not wait to conduct his own investigation, much like the character Old Sleuth in the dime-store novels he admired. The spirit of the detective overtook him, and he immediately offered his services to solve the homicide. He also changed his mind about the footprints after watching Arbios place Searcy's shoes into the prints leading away from the body.

The testimony and actions of T. F. Reardon had an undeniable impact in the case against Searcy. Even with his arrogant and abrasive personality, his testimony never wavered, and he produced the strongest evidence. The money he found in the vault area beneath the washroom was the most damning evidence for the prosecution, and its presence was inexplicable. Reardon had too much to lose, as his reputation meant everything—at least to himself. He had arrested Searcy, found the money, and summoned the district attorney and

Arbios back to the scene to conduct further investigation, which led to the filing of charges.

Three sheriff's deputies, J. L. Medlin from Daggett, J. J. Arbios from San Bernardino, and Frank Keyes from Needles, testified for the prosecution. Medlin and Keyes were desert-and-railroad-town deputies with experience dealing with crimes and residents along the railroad. Medlin lived in Daggett, and Keyes lived in Needles, which was a major railroad town. They were fearless and spent many years providing law-enforcement services in remote county areas.

Arbios, on the other hand, was a longtime deputy in San Bernardino who was paid to travel great distances to investigate the homicide. When he was called to the stand, his inexperience conducting investigations in the desert became obvious, and his credibility quickly faltered during questioning by the district attorney. He admitted he could not identify the points of the compass, and his lack of ability to recall the length of the footprint was alarming since he had all the while been claiming the footprints were a perfect match to the shoes belonging to Searcy. This testimony explains why he would spend more time on the stand than any other witness. He also testified he could not find the notes where he had written down the length of the prints. Cross-examination by Bledsoe and Willis was brutal and withering, and bystanders made fun of Arbios when he stepped off the witness stand and into the hall outside the courtroom, because he couldn't recall the points of the compass.

Eight physicians were called to either identify or dispute the presence of blood on Searcy's pants. Two of the physicians disputed the findings of blood corpuscles. Testimony from the physicians was boring and hardly earth-shattering as the ones who were convinced of the presence of blood could only identify blood corpuscles. The science of the time could not differentiate between human and animal blood corpuscles. In the end, the cumulative testimony of the physicians reflected questionable expertise. (By the latter part of the nineteenth century, there were 460 medical schools in the United States, and most were private enterprises.[79] Some of these educational institutions were more interested in making money than they were in the education of physicians.)

One of the doctors, Dr. C. A. McKechnie, accepted Searcy's pants for his scientific examination from Deputy Arbios at Lamb's Drug Store. McKechnie testified at the grand jury, and his testimony was the most questionable of all the doctors'. He was a graduate of the University of Glasgow, Scotland, and had been a practicing doctor and physician for twelve years. He swore he gained experience in the detection of blood during college and continued this study after his graduation. Bledsoe asked him specifically how many times he was called upon to examine fabrics where blood was present. His response was "twice," once in 1885 and again in 1890, 1891, or 1892; he was not sure of the year. He could not "enumerate" the other times he examined fabrics for blood. He claimed the power of a microscope could not be ascertained by knowing the diameter of the microscope.[80]

Doctor G. A. Rene, one of the expert witnesses who examined the pants, had the courage to "make a little statement" in which he questioned any physician's expertise and ability to identify blood in San Bernardino. Especially any testimony given by a physician weighed in a decision of the life or death of Searcy. In his mind, the evidence should not be used to potentially hang a man. Doctor Rene made a point of ensuring his argument was heard by everyone in the courtroom.

It was the prosecution's argument that Joseph Otto was murdered during the commission of a robbery because Searcy knew he was in possession of a large sum of money. To prove this point, the prosecution subpoenaed Ben L. Holmes, a resident of Needles and local agent of the Atlantic Pacific Railroad who was responsible for handing out payment to the railroad workers. He recalled paying Otto with two checks in the amounts of $21.10 and $12.50, with the last being a discharge ticket and not a full month's pay. Otto officially separated from the railroad and was paid around November 25, 1896. These discharge tickets were not uncommon, since sometimes the workers quit or were let go by the railroad. Holmes saw eighteen to twenty men, or sometimes forty, receive discharge tickets; sometimes on a regular payday, he could pay 120 to 125. The roadmaster dropped off the checks in Needles, which was the headquarters for the railroad. Holmes recalled that the check came back endorsed and presumed it was cashed in Needles. At one point, the victim was in possession of $33.60, but no one knew how much he spent before he was murdered four miles east of Bagdad.

Mrs. R. B. Weaver, the keeper of the section house at Danby, testified she had sold and fed the victim breakfast on Saturday morning, the day before his death. When it came time for payment, the victim reached into his pocket, removed a handful of change, and held it in his cupped hand. Using the fingers of the opposite hand, he moved the change around and removed a twenty-five-cent piece for payment. Mrs. Weaver could not see the denominations but was sure there were no gold coins in his cupped hand.

Joseph Otto was paid a total of $33.60 for two months' work, and he spent a week in Needles before starting his journey westbound on foot. In 1896 Needles was a thriving railroad and mining town with an abundance of stores, such as Monaghan and Murphy's, the Emporium of the Southwest, and saloons. There was no shortage of venues for Otto to spend his money in. The prosecution could not prove how much money he had in his possession when he was murdered, and the best a witness could testify was that he was careless when displaying his money.

The spirit of the detective moved T. F. Reardon to search for evidence of the crime when he located twenty-five dollars in the vault area of the water closet; part of the money was found under paper among the excrement, while another portion was in a slit separating two sections of the wooden structure. Deputy Sheriff J. J. Arbios was the premier witness for the prosecution, testifying longer than any other witness in the trial, and guessed at the direction of travel when he should have admitted he didn't know. Not to mention his questionable identification of the culprit's footprints. Doctor G. A. Rene was the only physician to profess the lack of expertise among physicians in San Bernardino who could positively identify blood corpuscles. He also cautioned the court that such evidence should not be taken lightly, considering the weight of the punishment was death by hanging.

On Tuesday, March 2, 1897, witness testimony ended. The following day, the prosecution and the defense began closing arguments to a packed courtroom. Each defense attorney gave eloquent closing arguments going into the evening. On Thursday, Gordan Hall was the last of the defense to speak, followed by the district attorney for rebuttal.

The case went to the jury on Thursday, March 4, at 3:45 p.m. and returned with a verdict at 4:30 p.m. The jury found Louis James Searcy guilty of murder in forty-five minutes without a punishment recommendation.

On April 5, 1897, Judge Oster sentenced Searcy to be hanged at San Quentin on June 25, 1897. The defense attorneys claimed they would "fight to the finish" and appealed the case.[81]

Handwritten note from the jury finding Louis James Searcy guilty of murder in the first degree (Courtesy of the San Bernardino County Assessor-Recorder-Clerk's office).

CHAPTER X

THE VIOLENCE CONTINUES

Well, Reardon, I've just received a telegram showing there's another murder out at Bagdad. You ought to be out there making another record for yourself with your arrests.
— Coroner A. C. Keating, February 27, 1897[82]

On Thursday, February 25, 1897, Johnie Moss, a Piute Indian and well-known medicine man, rode his horse into Bagdad in need of supplies. Known as Captain Johnie, he was working on a mining claim for Monohan and Murphy about fourteen miles northeast of the railroad settlement. Monohan and Murphy built the town of the Needles and maintained a store with ample supplies that Moss needed. Instead, Moss chose to visit Bagdad. (Saloons in the town of the Needles were not allowed to sell Native Americans alcohol, which may have helped his decision.) Moss was between forty-one and forty-three years of age, five-foot-three or-four, with a moustache, his hair combed back in a pompadour, and a dark complexion. Moss was intelligent, well-spoken, and well known throughout the region and was often mistakenly identified as Mexican because he spoke Spanish.

At 1:30 p.m. Moss entered Stewart's saloon, where William A. Ledbetter, an employee of J. A. Stewart and a monthlong resident of Bagdad, was tending the bar. He asked to buy bacon, flour, crackers, baking powder, and hay and grain for his horse. Ledbetter sold Moss all the supplies except for the bacon and flour, which he did not have on hand. During the transaction, Ledbetter made change for a ten-dollar gold piece, and when Moss opened his purse, he saw two twenty-dollar gold pieces. The forty dollars in his purse was about a month's wages for a resident living at Bagdad. Moss asked if he could move his horse to the corral behind the saloon to feed the animal, since he had left it by the Harvey House. Ledbetter obliged the tired traveler, who moved and tended to the horse, leaving it unattended in the corral.

At 2:30 p.m. Moss went on the hunt to buy more baking powder and stopped by the homes of Mrs. F. N. Honeywell and Mrs. Ellen Hess. Both women turned him down, indicating they had a limited supply and could only buy a pound at a time.

At 4:30 p.m. Moss returned to the saloon and asked what time Stewart would be back because he wanted to buy the bacon and flour and return home. Ledbetter told him Stewart would not be in until his arrival on the 6:00 p.m. train with additional supplies. Moss made a fatal error. He decided to wait for Stewart and have a drink that changed his life.

Jose Nunez, an unemployed Mexican contract laborer and Bagdad resident of two weeks, entered Stewart's saloon and bought a fifty-cent bottle of whiskey. Ledbetter knew Nunez well and had routinely sold him whiskey since his arrival; he thought it strange he never worked. Like a lot of Mexican contract laborers, Nunez followed work and had worked at several sidings along the Atlantic Pacific Railroad. This was his second stint at Bagdad after spending time at Franconia in the Territory of Arizona. Nunez had also lived in Jerome for five years and had spent time in Congress and Phoenix. He wasn't sure of his own age and thought he might be twenty-six or twenty-eight years old. He had come to the United States as a teenager with his father, who subsequently died, and he had no living relatives.

Nunez always paid cash for his whiskey, except for the day before, when he had pawned a revolver to Ledbetter for $1.50 and a bottle of whiskey. The three men—Ledbetter, Moss, and Nunez—stood at the bar. Moss and Nunez began to speak in Spanish, leaving Ledbetter out of the conversation. At one point, Nunez tried to sell Moss the pawned revolver, which Ledbetter had given to the men to inspect so they could haggle over a price. Moss declined and asked Ledbetter to show Nunez his own revolver, which he had been holding for payment for the hay and grain. After engaging in gunplay at the bar, the men returned the weapons to the saloonkeeper. The two men continued to speak, and after they each finished their drinks, Nunez collected his bottle of whiskey and Moss decided to buy a bottle of whiskey for himself. Before leaving, Nunez asked Ledbetter for another bottle for the pawned gun, and Ledbetter turned him down. Nunez then made for the door, but not before telling Moss something in Spanish.

Whatever Nunez told Moss was enough to entice him to follow him out of the saloon. The two strangers walked at a quick pace, with Moss trailing a few steps behind Nunez. The men walked northwest about 250 feet from the saloon, toward the Mexican area of the settlement. Moss entered the world of "Chihuahua," which the Mexican contractors called home. Unknown to Nunez, Moss left his horse unattended in the corral behind the saloon for everyone to see and, accordingly, question its owner's whereabouts.

The two slightly inebriated men walked toward the home of Francisco Maceo, a Mexican contract laborer who was then busy working at the coal chute. Maceo had no idea Nunez was taking Moss to his home with a promise of drunken entertainment. When the men entered the home, Gregorio Rede was drinking whiskey with Maceo's wife. Rede was no stranger to Bagdad and had lived there for a year and was a seven-year resident of California. Moss was excited to see the group of Nunez, Rede, and the woman drinking and carrying on. A fourth Mexican was playing a harp for the drunken crowd, who all sang along and danced. At 5:00 p.m. Francisco Maceo left work to run home to get some tobacco, and to his horror, he found the drunken group having a grand time at his residence. He quickly returned to the coal chute and asked his foreman if he could leave early because he had to deal with the mess he had discovered.

When he got back, Maceo found his wife in such a state that she could barely care for herself. He tried to calm her and get her into bed, but all the while, she kept trying to break away and go outside. He was angry at Nunez for bringing Moss to his home and drinking with his wife and the other men. Maceo was acquainted with Moss but still intent on getting everyone out. Before he could do that, Nunez signaled to Rede that Moss was in possession of a large amount of money and an easy target for a robbery.

At 5:30 p.m. Rede picked up a coal pickax with one hand and, with his other, grabbed one of Moss's wrists. He then swung the axe at Moss and landed a glancing blow below his nose with the flat side of the pick. Moss, awakening from his drunken haze and stinging from the strike, swung at Rede with a clenched fist and struck him above his eye, causing a small cut. Rede fell back, and once he recovered, he swung again and landed another blow, hitting

Moss below his nose, felling the victim. Maceo and his drunken wife watched the attack in slow motion, and he yelled at Rede to stop hurting the Indian. Rede told Maceo to shut up or he would kill both him and his wife. As Moss lay writhing on the floor, Rede switched to the pointed end of the pickax and landed a blow on the bridge of the nose, which violently threw Moss's head back, causing his neck to break. Maceo gathered his wife and fled the shack, passing Moss as he lay on the floor more dead than alive. To make sure Moss was dead, one of the men produced a revolver and shot him in the left side of the neck.

The lifeless body was bleeding out from the grotesque wounds. Rede tried to stop the blood by tightly wrapping Moss's head with one of his coats while Nunez closed all the doors and windows to the shack so no one could see the lifeless body. The two men searched the body. Rede, intoxicated and seemingly unaffected by the murder, took some of the victim's money and went to dinner at the Harvey House. John Testera, a railroad employee, saw him at the lunch counter and noticed he had blood on his left hand and a raw cut above his eye.

The murder of Johnie Moss didn't stop the good times at Bagdad. The drinking frenzy picked up immediately after the homicide and continued through Friday. Nunez, now flush with cash taken in the robbery/homicide, visited the saloon numerous times throughout Thursday and Friday to buy bottles of whiskey, and each time he paid in silver. J. A. Stewart questioned Nunez several times about the whereabouts of Johnie Moss, but he always shrugged off the inquiry, stating he didn't know. Stewart and the rest of the population of Bagdad didn't care much about the missing man except for the fact that he had left his horse unattended in the corral behind the saloon.

Rede and Nunez had a big problem, and that was what to do with the body of Johnie Moss. They tried to dispose of the body by loading it onto a freight train that stopped at Bagdad. A brakeman approached with a lantern, and the two quickly retreated, still carrying the body. The suspects then carried the body away from the train and discarded it twenty-one hundred feet away, under a creosote bush north of the settlement. Taking off their shoes and walking in their stockinged feet, the suspects circled over one thousand yards around the town to hide their route of travel.[83] They knew footprints were an important piece of evidence that could not be left behind.

The presence of the horse belonging to Johnie Moss in the corral could no longer be ignored. By Saturday, Stewart, hardly a representative of law and order, realized he had to do something and didn't want to bear any responsibility for the missing man. In his opinion, the Mexicans had done something to Moss or were holding him drunk against his will. That was fine because it was better to blame the Mexicans than his illegal drinking establishment. A party consisting of Mr. Dickenson, D. G. Rogers, Charles E. Boyd, and J. A. Stewart went looking for Moss, heading straight for the Mexican section of Bagdad. After searching five or six of the little buildings, they came to the home of Francisco Maceo, where Moss was last seen entering.

As the men entered the home, Francisco Maceo was nonchalantly grinding coffee while Gregoria Rede sat on the side of a bunk. The two men acted surprised when confronted, claiming Moss had come with Jose Nunez on Thursday and stayed for only a short time. Stewart asked where Jose was, and the men pointed to another bunk where Nunez was lying down and completely covered with a blanket from head to toe. Stewart pulled back the blanket: it was obvious Nunez was pretending to be asleep. Nunez claimed he had fallen asleep on Thursday and when he awoke, Moss was gone.

It was evident something was amiss, and the search party continued to look for the missing traveler. They figured if Moss had run afoul of the Mexicans, his body would have been carried north up the natural incline. It was now eleven in the morning, and the search party started walking down the track and looking in all directions. They could see quite a few Mexicans leaving their tie houses and watching the group as they searched for Moss. The group started up the incline by the tie houses, found a faint trail, and then saw an object behind a group of greasewoods. As they walked toward the object, the victim's foot came into focus, and then the whole body. The head was wrapped tightly in a coat; there was so much coagulated and dried blood soaked into the jacket that it was stuck to the victim's face. The jacket had to be pried away to see the victim's face and gruesome injuries.

Mr. Boyd telegraphed the coroner and tried to contact the deputy sheriff in Daggett but learned he was away in San Bernardino. The fact was, J. L. Medlin was in San Bernardino, where he was testifying at the trial of Louis James Searcy! The search party rounded up Rede and Nunez and awaited the arrival of the authorities. By now, Rede had developed a black eye after being struck by Moss during the homicide. Deputy Keyes received word in Needles, responded to the scene, and conducted the investigation. Keyes discovered that the suspects had torn up part of the bloodstained wood flooring and burned it but had still left blood evidence. He also found the axe used in the murder in the backyard of the shack.[84]

On February 28, 1897, the day after the discovery of the body, A. C. Keating convened a morning session of a coroner's inquest at Bagdad. Present were Deputy Keyes, Assistant District Attorney L. M. Sprecher, and a jury of F. C. Kenyon, C. E. Boyd, John Testera, A. Dressing, Charles St. Clair, W. A. Ledbetter, D. G. Rogers, F. Honeywell, and of course, J. A. Stewart. The inquest was convened to determine the cause of death of Johnie Moss, and the body was available for everyone to inspect. Coroner Keating started the inquiry, after which C. E. Boyd, a juror, made a statement based on his own observations and detective work. Before the coroner's inquest, he made a point of matching the murder weapon to the injuries on the victim's body.

"The pick here this morning, as I picked it up, I thought I would see if it fit the wound in the head, and I took it over and tried it, and I placed the third corner on the wound in the head here in this direction like that, not pressing it down any more that the weight of the pick would be, and fit it, and that may be where the blood came on to the end of the pick."

Keating also shared his observation about a bullet wound on the left side of the victim's neck. The wound came from a .32- or .38-caliber pistol ball and may have severed an artery, and it was a "good clean gunshot wound." Witnesses also testified they saw Rede wearing the jacket that was used to wrap Moss's head and noted the fact he was also short of money at the time of the homicide. B. F. Butler, an agent and operator for the railroad company and resident of Bagdad, testified Rede had not worked on the coal chute for three weeks and his last paycheck was for forty-three dollars on January 27. Maceo, confronted with all the evidence, admitted seeing Rede murder Moss in his home. Rede and Nunez were brought back to San Bernardino and charged with the murder of Johnie Moss.

Later, Moss's wife came to town looking for him, viewed the body, and showed the least of emotion over it. But upon leaving, she remarked, "Someone has done this. There is a good Indian law—a tooth for a tooth—I am going back; I go now." She started out immediately for her tribe, about fifty miles distant, and about what the outcome would be there was no doubt as she could raise the necessary number of men to avenge the death—"a tooth for a tooth."

There were a great many vagrant Mexicans hanging around Bagdad who lived on the few who had work, and after the murder, there was a stampede of all who could get away.

"Coroner Keating took a good coffin, and they gave the dead man a decent burial."[85]

On March 10, 1897, Rede and Nunez were charged with the murder of Captain Johnie Moss, as witnessed by a crowded courtroom of spectators. The prosecution was conducted by assistant district attorneys, and the defense was headed by C. L. Allison and C. B. Morris and looked after by B. F. Bledsoe.[86,87] Exactly two months following Moss's murder, on April 25, 1897, Gregorio Rede was convicted of second-degree murder and sentenced to ten years to life.[88] Once the jury was impaneled, Jose Nunez pleaded guilty to accessory after the fact and was sentenced to five years in state prison. He had originally been charged with murder.[89] At the end of the trial and sentencing, there were no appeals, fanfare, or lengthy press coverage.

J. A. Stewart continued to run his illegal saloon, which more than likely continued to fuel violent crime. On March 19, 1898, Sheriff Holcomb received a strange telegraph that read, "I will kill Stewart tonight, if he comes out of his place tonight. Chas Elliot." Holcomb sent a warning dispatch to Stewart and ordered Deputies Medlin and Keyes to respond to Bagdad to investigate. Deputy Keyes wrote a letter to Holcomb describing what he discovered:

I came to Bagdad this morning on the first train that came after I received your message and have investigated the matter of Chas Elliott sending you the telegram informing you that he was going to kill J. A. Stewart. I find that he, Eliott, had been working with Crowley's grading gang and had come to Bagdad and got full of whiskey. He had been lying outside somewhere drunk for some hours and when he got up, he claimed that he had been "rolled" and blamed Stewart for it, then, without saying a word to Stewart about being "rolled" or anything else, went to the telegraph office and wired you as he did. But he has not been seen or heard of since. Stewart had not heard of Elliott's threat until your message came informing him. There is, I think, four or five hundred men working on the railroad near here, and will be for six or eight weeks yet, and many of them are said to be tough characters. There is liable and apt to be serious trouble here at any time. The agent here and others say they think there ought to be a deputy sheriff or two here to help keep peace. I told them I thought you would appoint someone, but it seems no one wants the job.[90]

Either directly or indirectly, Stewart continued to have a negative impact on the tiny population of Bagdad. On Friday, April 1, 1898, Geronimo Delgardo stabbed Avanico Gonzalez in the stomach during a drunken brawl.[91] On Sunday, April 3, Sheriff Holcomb brought Delgardo in from Bagdad and arrested him for assault to kill. Delgardo quickly pled guilty to a lesser charge of assault with a deadly weapon and was sentenced to two years at San Quentin.[92] The entire case was adjudicated in less than a week, and Delgardo was sent off to state prison.

From December 1896 to April 1898, there were six violent crimes surrounding the illegal saloon belonging to J. A. Stewart in Bagdad, with a population of only twenty-five to thirty individuals. There were three homicides, two assaults with a deadly weapon, and one robbery. J. A. Stewart was the suspect in 50 percent of the crimes but was never arrested. The four arrests made were of three Mexicans and one biracial African American.

Date	Crime	Victim	Suspect(s)	Sentence
January 26, 1896	Assault with a deadly weapon	Unknown	J. A. Stewart	Not arrested
January 27, 1896	Homicide	Jose Lopez	J. A. Stewart	Not arrested (justifiable)
December 6, 1896	Murder	Joseph Otto	Louis James Searcy	Sentenced to Death
February 25, 1897	Murder / accessory after the fact	Johnie Moss	Gregorio Rede, Jose Nunez	Ten years (San Quentin), Five years (San Quentin)
March 19, 1898	Robbery	Chas Elliot	J. A. Stewart	Not arrested / victim not at the scene
April 1, 1898	Assault with a deadly weapon	Avanico Gonzalez	Geronimo Delgardo	Two years (San Quentin)

*Courtesy of California
State Archives*

CHAPTER XI

THE APPEAL
LOUIS JAMES SEARCY

Searcy and his attorneys stood in front of the court when the guilty verdict was read aloud. The attorneys dropped their heads, and after a moment of silence and self-pity, they consoled Searcy and promised him they would not give up.

They had fought so hard during the trial with determined and pointed cross-examination that they figured a not-guilty verdict was a given. In their minds, they had proven certain witnesses exaggerated or lied beyond a reasonable doubt and so proven their client's innocence to the jury. The guilty verdict was devastating for their client and their own self-worth. Searcy stood unmoved by the verdict as he was a "chance spectator to the scene" and he didn't seem to be affected in the least. He asked his attorneys not to divulge any of his personal information because he did not want his elderly mother to know of his arrest and fate. He also asked his attorneys to draw up his will, saying, "I have only $1.55 in the world, which they took from me when I was arrested. It is mine, honestly mine, and it is all I have in the world, and I wish to leave it to you. It is not much, but it may remind you of your struggles to save the life of an innocent man."[93]

Their dedication while working pro bono was recognized by the local newspaper: "From start to finish they [defense attorneys] have made a gallant fight, and their speeches to the jury were listened to by a crowded courtroom, drawn there through the interest in the young men who had taken the case without fee or reward, other than the plaudits and words of praise of their friends. In this they were not disappointed, for their work has earned them many congratulatory remarks."[94] Bledsoe and Hall wasted no time and began working on the appeal as their client was set to be hung at San Quentin prison on June 25. In 1897 the criminal justice system moved quickly, and the attorneys went to work trying to save Searcy's life. Willis departed the defense team and returned to his own legal practice in the Territory of Arizona.

On March 15, eleven days after the verdict and the same day as sentencing, Bledsoe and Hall filed two separate motions. Bledsoe filed a motion for a new trial on the grounds that 1) the jury learned Searcy was wanted for burglary in Prescott, 2) the jury was guilty of misconduct, 3) the court misdirected the jury in the matters of law, 4) the court erred in the decisions in the questions of law, 5) the verdict was contrary to the law, and 6) the verdict was contrary to the evidence.

Hall filed a lengthy motion for a new trial and described the trial and the role it played in daily life in the City of San Bernardino. In his affidavit, he described what he saw during his walk between the courthouse and his office. He recognized the names and the faces of the jurors and witnesses who came from distant places and were forced to stay in the city. At the end of each day of court proceedings, they sought out forms of entertainment. If you came from the far-off railroad settlements, it was a treat to be around and interact with other people and San Bernardino was an exciting and bustling railroad city. This was probably the first time some of them had been in San Bernardino, and they remained in the city for the entire or greater part of the ten-day trial.

According to Hall, the case was so well known it caused gossip and discussion in and around the city, at places of "public resort" outside of the courthouse. The people on the jury and witnesses mingled with each other without restriction except with the court's formal admonishment. Hall wrote in his affidavit that he heard groups of men made up of sworn prosecution witnesses who were called in from Danby, Amboy, and Bagdad discussing the evidence of the case and giving their opinions as to the guilt of the defendant. He also swore he saw witnesses and jurors openly discussing opinions that were prejudicial and damaging to the defendant, as well as the jury foreman engaging in these conversations.[95] He provided specific details of jury misconduct on two separate days.

On Saturday, February 27, during a recess at the time of the trial, Hall claimed to have seen jurors Jacob Anderson, Joseph Bessant, and Clifton Hill sitting on the east steps of the courthouse openly and improperly discussing their testimony and rendering opinions on aspects of the trial. Hill was talking to the group, and he was commenting and telling the men about the positioning of the body and the condition of the footprints at the crime scene. He also discussed a specific response he made under cross-examination as to why he didn't approach the body. Hall swore he heard Hill say, "Why you bet I didn't want to stay there long, or examine the body, because it's a mighty ticklish thing to come upon a dead body all alone out there in that country." Reardon then chimed in and bragged about his arrest of the defendant at gunpoint.

At this point, Dr. A. C. Keating, coroner of San Bernardino County, walked toward the group of witnesses holding a telegram and told Reardon in full earshot of everyone, "Well, Reardon, I've just received a telegram showing there's been another murder out at Bagdad. You ought to be out there making another record for yourself with your arrests."

Reardon replied, "Yes, that's so, but I can't be out there and here too. I can't fix more than one of those fellows at the same time." This was the telegraph notifying the coroner that Rede and Nunez were under arrest for the murder of Johnie Moss.

Hall ended his affidavit by stating, "By reason of the character, notoriety, and publicity given the said trial, the jury sworn to try this cause were precluded from rendering a fair and impartial verdict."[96]

Then on March 1, three days before the verdict, Hall was walking with Mr. J. McBrown when the men passed the Exchange Saloon on Third Street and saw three of the four men standing in front having a discussion. As they passed the group, someone uttered the words "Oh! That nigger killed the Dutchman all straight up." Hall said that the jury foreman, Joseph Bessant, Esq., was standing close enough that he should have heard the statement. It was the opinion of Hall that "said remark was of such a character and spoken in such a manner as would naturally influence, bias, and prejudice said juryman against said defendant."

As a result of the motion, District Attorney Daley was forced to track down witnesses Clifton Hill, Conrad Stumpf, and Joseph Bessant and interview them. All the men provided a sworn and signed written statement denying they ever heard any such comments.[97]

This wasn't the end, as the defense made more allegations of jury and witness commingling and misconduct, which the prosecution was forced to address. On March 20 the prosecution filed an affidavit signed by witnesses for the prosecution of Clifton Hill and Conrad Stumpf. The witnesses swore they had casually met a juror, Jacob Anderson, at Third and D Streets. The men spoke for a brief time, and Hill said he was going to buy a ticket for the opera house. This seemed like a good idea, as they were all strangers to the city. Stumpf and Anderson were German, and the two men were enjoying speaking in their native tongue. Stumpf and Anderson asked Hill if he could buy them a ticket as well. Stumpf handed Hill fifty cents, and Anderson gave him twenty cents. Hill reminded Anderson the tickets were thirty cents, so Stumpf offered to pay the ten-cent difference. The men went to the opera house and enjoyed a night of entertainment but swore they never discussed the case. Anderson denied he was the guest of the two witnesses.[98]

On March 29, 1897, at ten o'clock in the morning, court was back in session, and it was the time and place to hear contra affidavits filed by the district attorney. Bledsoe and Hall were present, representing their client, the district attorney read the contra affidavits, and both sides argued their case. According to the contra affidavits filed by the district attorney, all the witnesses denied any wrongdoing. They denied the conversations ever took place and denied hearing the remarks submitted to the court by Bledsoe and Hall. The denials could only mean one thing: Hall and Bledsoe had lied about overhearing specific details included in their filings. This included hearing T. F. Reardon bragging about his arrest of Searcy and comments made by Clifton Hill.

On April 5, 1897, Judge Oster denied the motion for a new trial and ruled the district attorney acted in good faith when he told the jury Searcy was fleeing from another crime and the conversations between jurors and witnesses were inconclusive. Judge Oster sentenced Searcy to death by hanging at San Quentin State Prison on June 25, 1897.

On April 6, 1897, Bledsoe and Hall appealed to the California Supreme Court, which stayed the execution. The defense attorneys then requested Searcy be sent to San Quentin until the California Supreme Court heard the case in October. This made the most sense, as the climate in San Francisco was milder and conditions in state prison were much better than in county jail. Searcy was then transferred to San Quentin in the company of Jessie Case, a jailer, and Sheriff Holcomb. The sheriff would only accompany Searcy until Mojave, where he would depart to carry out business in Randsburg.[99] If and when the appeal was to be heard, Searcy would return to San Bernardino for resentencing.

On June 5, 1897, twenty days before the scheduled execution, Bledsoe and Hall filed a bill of exceptions, which further delayed the execution,[100] and continued to represent Searcy at no cost based on their belief that he was innocent. On May 28, 1898, the California Supreme Court affirmed the decision of the Superior Court of San Bernardino, and the date of execution stood.

After spending fifteen months at San Quentin, Searcy was returned to San Bernardino, where Judge Oster once again sentenced him to be executed at San Quentin. Upon leaving for San Quentin's death row, with a new execution date of October 7, 1898, Searcy thanked the court and continued to insist he was innocent. The daily logbook at San Quentin, dated July 18, 1998, documents the return of "Louis James Searcy, (Negro), Death, Murder 1st Degree, from San Bernardino, Returned from resentence and the weather was fair and windy." Although he was sentenced to death, a hint of his innocence was written by an unknown columnist for the *San Bernardino County Sun*: "He [Searcy] protests his innocence but with few to believe him, although the testimony was purely circumstantial and would have fitted any other man if he had happened along at the time of the murder."

By September 17, 1898, Bledsoe had appealed to the governor for clemency and to commute the sentence to life imprisonment. Judge Oster, who sentenced Searcy to death twice, wrote the governor asking for a commutation of the sentence, which was followed by a petition from the public.[101] On October 6, 1898, one day before Searcy was scheduled to be executed, B. F. Bledsoe received a telephone message from Governor Budd's office that Searcy's sentence had been commuted to life in prison. A point of contention was the identification of tracks leading from where the victim was murdered, with two witnesses swearing they were made by Searcy despite them having not seen the prints until a week after the murder.[102]

CHAPTER XII

PRISON
SAN QUENTIN

The State of California housed its first state prison inmates aboard an old ship called the *Waban*, anchored in the San Francisco Bay. In 1852 the California state legislature authorized the purchase of twenty acres of land at Point San Quentin, located across the bay from San Francisco in Marin County. The prison ship was then towed to Point San Quentin, and the forty or fifty prisoners completed construction of the prison in 1854.[103]

Louis James Searcy arrived at San Quentin State Prison on April 9, 1897; he was issued inmate number 17259. He was interviewed and photographed, and his hair and moustache were shaved off so he would resemble the rest of the inmate population. His intake photograph indicated his race was "Negro." He stood out in the inmate population, as most were Caucasian, interspersed with Chinese, Mexicans, and a few Japanese. The chalkboard by his photograph indicated "Murder 1st Degree, San Bernardino, to be executed June 25, 1897."

Ironically, the next day, another inmate was received at San Quentin. William H. T. Durrant, or Theodore Durrant, inmate number 17260, went through the same process, and the chalkboard by his photo indicated he was "to be executed June 11, 1897." He was convicted of murdering two women in 1895 and hiding one of the bodies in a church belfry and the other in a closet. The media dubbed him the "Demon of the Belfry." On November 11, 1897, Durrant was granted a reprieve from his death sentence. "This day a stay of execution on writ for probable cause and was taken from death chamber at 7 p.m. and confined in cell 21."[104] His stay of execution was short-lived, and on January 7, 1898, Durrant, in prison for murder in the first degree, was executed and discharged from the custody of San Quentin State Prison. The weather that day was fair/cold. Durrant's story garnered much more attention before and long after Searcy's time at San Quentin.

A prison board of directors met monthly and provided oversight for San Quentin and Folsom, California's two state prisons, and the minutes were captured in large minute books. Most board items discussed were contracts for supplies and the purchase of materials such as coal. The meetings also covered some noteworthy events such as violations of prison rules, inmate punishment, or inmates who were declared insane, and the warden provided a report of all executions within San Quentin's prison walls. Interestingly, logged in these minutes is the mention that Levi Strauss was a supplier of clothing to the prison.

A daily logbook documented everyday life in San Quentin, which included inmate counts, weather, movement of inmates facing execution, inmate entertainment, and violation of prison rules. The population of prison inmates when Searcy arrived was 1,316 and included a small number of women. Searcy's twelve years of incarceration were filled with death, inmate violence, drug smuggling and use, mental illness, escape attempts, and prison riots. Drugs were nothing new, and as early as 1800, doctors and pharmacists were promoting the pain-relieving properties of opium with little regard for abuse or addiction.[105]

Death sentences were frequent and spoken about among prisoners; they included an audience of invited spectators and were typically carried out at 10:30 a.m. Sometimes the inmates facing their sentences gave a few last words or faced death with a smile on their faces. Death didn't always come at the end of a rope. On May 27, 1907, prisoner Fred C. Grant "was caught in machinery at the mill and horribly mutilated surviving his injuries until this afternoon and he died in the p.m."[106]

Inmate violence was always a part of prison life, as well as mental illness, and several times a year, inmates were declared insane and transferred to the Stockton Insane Asylum. On December 11,

103

1897, Harvey Nolan, prisoner identification number 15646, lost one year of credit after cutting a fellow inmate with a knife.[107] On November 12, 1898, Lillie Bager, prisoner identification number 16504, was examined and, according to law, found to be insane and transferred to Stockton Insane Asylum.[108] On December 10, 1904, Roft Garner, prisoner identification number 19611, was found in possession of a knife and found guilty; a judge ordered that Garner be sentenced to five days with only bread and water.[109] On April 20, 1905, twelve prisoners who were confined to the incorrigible cells started an impetuous riot. "They yelled and screamed and broke from their fastenings the cast iron water closets in their cells which they broke to pieces. The guards succeeded in quieting them by threatening to turn on the fire hose into their cell and they were placed on a bread and water diet."[110]

Like in all prisons, inmates wanted to escape their confines. On December 16, 1898, Stanislaus Voniakorsky, prisoner identification number 17006, "attempt[ed] escape by cutting out the roof of his cell" and he forfeited all his credits earned."[111] On March 8, 1905, prisoner Johnson, identification number 20650, "attempted to escape by concealing himself in the rear of the jute mill and was discovered missing by Captain Harrison at lock up. Grounds and jute mill were searched, and convict found in a very few minutes. Johnson was placed in the dungeon and charged with attempted escape were placed against him. Claims he went to sleep in the jute mill."[112] On August 27, 1906, four inmates who had recently been transferred from Folsom "were for several days past acting in a suspicious manner; today Captain of Guards E. V. Ellis went to Shepards Point and with a field glass watched their movements and thus unearthed the plot. They were engaged in making water and airtight diving suits in which they planned to escape. The quartet was removed to the dungeon." The inmate population was then 1,567.

Prisoner punishment included being placed in a dungeon or having movement restricted by straitjackets.

Narcotic use was also prevalent in San Quentin. On August 14, 1897, John O'Rourke, prisoner identification number 15519, was found to be in possession of opium and forfeited eighteen months of credit, but the board returned eleven of said eighteen months.[113] On September 9, 1899, "bringing opium into the prison—by order of the court Loy Perez, Serial 16280 and Walter Furnish, 17817 were taken to San Rafael to answer charges brought against them for breaking Section 180 of the Penal Code (i.e. bringing opium into the prison and sentenced to 1 year commencing this day)."[114] The standing prison population was then 1,300. On December 5, 1903, three Mexican inmates were caught bringing opium into the prison and had a preliminary examination before a magistrate and were bound over to the superior court under $2,000 bail each.[115]

As evidenced by the above episodes, life was cheap and fragile in San Quentin. Still, it was not without some level of compassion shown by the warden. There were bands that played for the inmate population, and lemonade was served all day on the Fourth of July. At one point, a barbershop opened to serve inmates. An inmate broke out of the incorrigible cell and ran into the barbershop and grabbed a razor. He then ran into the yard and sliced himself under the threat of being shot. The day after this incident, the barbershop was closed.

On November 26, 1903, "entertainment was given during the day by the S. Q. Minstrel and Vaudeville Company, 3 hours of entertainment and an elaborate holiday menu was served. The minstrel company repeated their entertainment for the benefit of the officers and guards of the prison and their friends and relatives. The warden showed his appreciation of the boys' efforts by presenting them with several boxes of cigars."[116] Inmates were offered a Christmas dinner, and the one celebrated on December 25, 1907, stood out: "Splendid Christmas dinner served in the general mess hall at 2 p.m. Many old timers say it was the best meal ever served there. Band played in yard at 11 a.m. and 1 p.m." It was forty-six degrees and raining at San Quentin the day of the celebration, and the inmate population was growing. It now stood at 1,594 inmates.

On April 19, 1906, at 5:12 a.m., the San Francisco earthquake shook San Quentin prison, but there is no record of deaths or major destruction. San Quentin was just coming to life in preparation for another day, and Searcy, locked in a prison cell, had nowhere to flee during the violent quake. Anyone able to look out toward San Francisco would have seen the smoke from fires burning throughout the city. The impact on the prison was the loss of contractors who supplied the prison with necessities. A State Prison Directors meeting was held on May 17, 1906, to discuss the action needed to keep the prison functioning. "Most of the contractors furnishing supplies were in San Francisco and the late fire and earthquake destroyed their buildings and stock of goods. Warden authorizes to purchase supplies in open market the contractors cannot comply with the contracts in the future."[117]

A year before Searcy's release, an unexpected court proceeding took place in Judge Oster's courtroom: On January 5, 1907, in the Superior Court of San Bernardino County, Judge Oster ordered the release of the twenty-five dollars found by T. F. Reardon eleven years earlier in the vault area of the washhouse at Danby, which was in the possession of the court as an exhibit in the homicide trial. The court identified the money as the property of T. F. Reardon and directed it to be released to B. F. Bledsoe. The order of the court was for Bledsoe to deliver the money to Reardon with the understanding the court did not recognize the money belonged to Searcy. The stipulation indicated the money "is the property of T. F. Reardon and it is hereby stipulated that the court herein may make an order directing the said Clerk to deliver to same Benjamin F. Bledsoe who shall receipt for the same in the name of T. F. Reardon and deliver the same the said T. F. Reardon." The order was signed by Judge Oster, Benjamin F. Bledsoe, and F. B. Daley, and on January 10, B. F. Bledsoe acknowledged receipt of the money.[118]

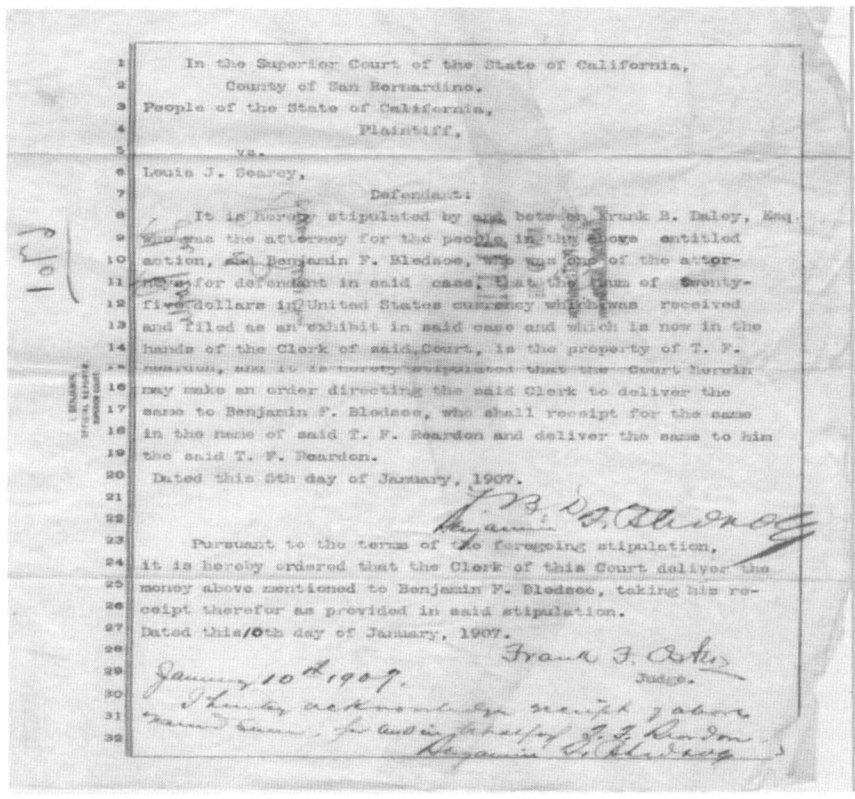

Court order signed by Judge Oster, dated January 5, 1907, authorizing the release of the twenty-five dollars found by T. F. Reardon to Benjamin F. Bledsoe. On January 10, 1907, Bledsoe acknowledged receipt of the money on behalf of Reardon (Courtesy of the San Bernardino County Assessor-Recorder-Clerk's office).

On page 334 of the prisoners' daily logbook for San Quentin, dated July 14, 1908, it is noted that Louis James Searcy was paroled. The word "negro" was written in red by his name, and after serving more than twelve years, he was released from San Quentin. This was his first day of freedom since T. F. Reardon had stopped the handcar east of Danby on December 7, 1896, pointed a Winchester rifle at him, and detained him as a proclaimed citizen of the United States. As he entered California, he traveled on foot from Needles and passed through small settlements dotting the railroad—places like Fenner, Homer, Danby, Amboy, and finally Bagdad. These places may as well have been a million miles away from the gates of San Quentin when Searcy was discharged from the prison and released on parole.

Notably, an inmate was granted parole because his prison life had been commendable. Pardons would then be granted, upon a recommendation of the board of prison directors, to all paroled prisoners who behaved themselves outside of the prison walls.[119]

On July 17, 1908, the *San Bernardino County Sun* ran an article on the second page titled "Long Fight to Secure Liberty: Man [Searcy] Convicted of Murder in First Degree Gains His Liberty After a Contest Covering Twelve Years." The author describes the trial as "one of the hottest legal fights this county ever witnesses to cheat the gallows, is again at liberty. After facing the hangman's noose for months, being twice sentenced to death, and having been an inmate of San Quentin for a period of twelve years." In order to prepare for the story, the author reviewed the court file, which included all of the affidavits filed by the defense attorneys. The article ended by saying, "The outcome of the trial was to obtain a commutation of the sentence, reducing it to life imprisonment. And now, after 12 long years, Searcy had again a chance to make a man of himself."[120]

CHAPTER XIII
REDDING

Tried so hard to explain

The way things are and how quick they can change

But you never listened you just turned your head

Never even heard a single word that he said

While it's true now that I'm not a saint

I felt pain when you live to hate

Said it before and I'll say it again

Leave me alone man or treat me like a friend

I had a dream last night

Everybody's laughing and everything was alright

Still some hope in sight, that was last night

I had a dream last night

Nobody's crying, nobody's frightened

Still some hope in sight, that was last night

Well if it seems like I sound like the rest

We're trying hard not to be too depressed

Once they take everything I've left, it's so easy

So if you're dreaming I hope that you do

Wish for the best and hope that it comes true

Who knows what they'll leave when they're through

I had a dream last night

Everybody's laughing and everything was alright

Still some hope in sight, that was last night

I had a dream last night

Nobody's crying, nobody's frightened

Still some hope in sight, that was last night

—*The Long Ryders, "I Had a Dream"*[121]

In 1908 Searcy stepped off a train in the City of Redding, in Northern California, which sits along the Sacramento River. Located 162 miles north of Sacramento, in the shadows of the Mount Lassen Volcano, it would be the perfect place for Searcy to call home.

His life was always shaped by the railroad in some manner, and this move was no exception. The construction of the Central Pacific Railroad in 1872 created the town originally called Poverty Flats. Public lots went up for sale, and within a month, twenty-three buildings were under construction and a hundred lots had been sold. Fifteen short years after its creation, the city incorporated in 1887, and by the next year, Redding became the seat for Shasta County. The copper-mining industry added to the economic growth of Redding, and by 1910, it had reached its peak, with fourteen mines and six major smelters. The city now had a new high school, four elementary schools, seven hotels, two daily and three weekly newspapers, and a population of about five thousand. There were also two banks with over $2 million in deposits and the largest department store north of Sacramento.[122]

Before his incarceration, Searcy had been accustomed to settling into new places with ease, and the small and economically stable community was a perfect place to call home. His likable and soft-spoken personality made it easy for him to find a job; he was a perfect employee.

On June 21, 1910, at the age of fifty-one, after two years on parole, Searcy completed an application for executive clemency, which shared intimate background about his life. His eighty-five-year-old mother was living in Los Angeles and was dependent on his support. He had not heard from other members of his family in thirty years and thought they were all dead. Born into slavery in Kentucky, he was six years old at the end of the Civil War.

MT. LASSEN IN ERUPTION CAN BE SEEN FROM THE WINDOWS OF THIS HOTEL

HOTEL LORENZ. REDDING, CAL.
ARTHUR L. WATSON, MGR.

While on parole, he held jobs with the Pullman Company, Wagner Palace Car Company, and the Hoyle and Lorenz Hotels. He would spend most of his life in Redding, working at or around the Lorenz Hotel.

The last part of the application was a summary of why he should be granted a pardon: "Innocent of the crime for which convicted, and a victim of circumstances. All papers relating to my case are on file in the State Prison at San Quentin, California. Have been on parole for two years." He referenced his defense attorneys Judge Benjamin F. Bledsoe, Senator H. M. Willis, and Gordon Hall. After the trial, his attorneys moved on to successful careers, with Bledsoe and Willis becoming the most notable.

On July 30, 1910, the state board of prison directors wrote a letter to Governor James N. Gillett:

WHEREAS, Convict No. 17259, Louis James Searcy sentenced from San Bernardino County to serve a term of life for the crime of murder of the first degree, received at this prison April 9, 1897, was paroled according to the law on July 14, 1908, and WHEREAS, said Convict No. 17259, Louis James Searcy was confined in the State Prison at San Quentin for more than eleven years prior to his parole, and since his release on parole he has at all time conducted himself in a most exemplary manner and the State Board of Prison Directors considers him worthy of executive clemency, NOW, THEREFORE, BE IT RESOLVED, that the State Board of Prison Directors does respectfully recommend to His Excellency, the Governor of California, that said Convict No. 17259, Louis J. Searcy be pardoned.[123]

His pardon was granted, and he was released of all liabilities to the State of California and San Bernardino County. Amboy, Bagdad, Cadiz, Danby, and San Bernardino were memories of far-off places and pieces of an unimaginable nightmare.

Searcy moved on with his life and was employed during special events in the community, attended by well-known Redding residents. Life in Redding consisted of hard work and friendships interspersed with a handful of vacations, fishing opportunities, and civic duties.

The local newspaper reported community events and often included the names of residents—Searcy routinely appeared in a positive light.

One lighthearted reference in the newspaper conveys his peaceful existence in Redding. On August 6, 1911, Louis James Searcy accompanied Miss Alice Firth, Miss Carrie Neilson, Warren Reese, and Mr. and Mrs. John P. Irish on a trip to Manzanita Lake. They would spend two weeks on a camping trip. He looked after the commissary department.[124] Manzanita Lake was and still is a popular fishing and family destination for local travelers, and during this trip, there was a report of swarms of butterflies that a month before had been swarms of caterpillars.[125] It is hard to imagine the delight Searcy had in this sight after being incarcerated for so many years.

Throughout his entire time at Redding, it was clear Searcy always worked hard and was an active member of the community. In August 1911 "one hundred and seventy-five invited guests enjoyed the splendid hospitality of Mrs. Emma Hoyle Saturday evening at the Hotel Lorenz where elegantly gowned matrons and maids representative of the most prominent families in Redding and other parts of Shasta County between 9 and 12 o'clock. The brilliant function evidenced rare judgement on the part of the hostess in its carefully detailed arrangement. The ballroom was tastefully decorated with evergreens and flowers and a buffet was arranged in the rear of the room where crushed fruit punch was served to the many guests by James Searcy the caterer."[126]

In July1916 Searcy departed for San Francisco and Los Angeles, spent four weeks on a vacation, and considered taking a trip to Seattle before returning home.[127] The front page of the *Shasta Courier*, dated May 24, 1918, read, "Every Man of Draft Age Must Work or Fight After July 1." The front page also carried a story about local contributions to the Red Cross war fund; Searcy donated five dollars.[128] He participated in fishing, as previously mentioned, and in 1919 he was first in line to obtain his fishing license.[129] The same year he departed on a two-month vacation in the mountains of Eastern Shasta and Siskiyou Counties.[130]

By 1923 Searcy had given up his attempts at running a bootblack stand on Market Street and resumed his old job at the Lorenz Hotel. For fifteen years, he had been the accommodating porter of that hostelry before embarking in business for himself.[131] The *Sacramento Bee* carried another interesting article about Searcy's mother. "Mother, 99, Still Addresses Son, 66, as 'My Baby Boy.' 'Jimmie' as the porter is known by the traveling public, writes to his mother every week without fail, and he as often receives a letter from her."[132]

In 1930 a funeral was held for Frank Alexander, a well-known and wealthy African American in Redding, with scores of friends crowding the McDonald and Scott Chapel and the casket banked high with beautiful flowers. Funeral services were conducted in the afternoon. Reverend E. M. Clark, pastor of the A. M. E. Zion Church, and Reverend J. M. Cherry officiated. Searcy was a pall-bearer.[133]

On January 26, 1934, Harold Emory was driving to work when he saw someone face down in the middle of the street at California and Gold Streets. Like in Clifton Hill's discovery of Joseph Otto four miles east of Bagdad, he thought the person was asleep. He walked up to the body and shook him and saw he was dead. Louis James Searcy had died in the middle of the street in Redding as he walked to work as a janitor at the Elks Lodge.

An obituary in the *Record Searchlight* read:

James Searcy Passes Suddenly—James Searcy, 75, well known colored man of Redding was found dead on the street near California and Gold Streets early Saturday morning. He had suffered a heart attack Friday night and was taken to a hospital but recovered sufficiently to return to his room in the Lincoln House the same evening. Heart failure is believed to have ended his life as he started downtown for his days work. Searcy came to Redding in 1906 and had resided here since. He was for many years a porter at the Hotel Lorenz, later operating a bootblack stand in the Houses Barber shop. Of recent years he was a janitor for the Elks and other Redding buildings.[134]

Funeral services for Searcy were held on a Tuesday afternoon at 3:30 p.m. in the McDonald and Scott Chapel, with Reverand P. T. Coleman officiating. The burial was made in the Redding Cemetery.[135]

Louis "Jimmy" Searcy rests at the Redding Cemetery in lot number three, space number three, in an unmarked grave. He knew his time would eventually come, so he bought his own grave site. The twenty-six years he spent in Redding were peaceful, and there is no evidence anyone knew or cared about his time on death row, the time he spent incarcerated at San Quentin State Prison, or the gallant legal battle his young attorneys waged. His life was a simple one, with no further contacts with the law or complaints about his behavior or allegations of theft. It was identical to his time living in Phoenix, where proprietors trusted him with large sums of money and the care of their businesses. His behavior while in prison and on parole was exemplary. One would expect the behavior of a person who committed a violent homicide to manifest itself before and after the crime. But throughout his entire life, Searcy's behavior was that of a small-statured, soft-spoken, harmless man with a severe stutter.

Thirty-eight years before Searcy passed away, two unemployed Mexican contract laborers living at Bagdad most likely murdered Joseph Otto four miles east of the settlement. The suspects were out of work and needed money for more whiskey and food. Maybe still drunk from the night before, they walked east from Bagdad before sunrise, looking for a victim to rob. Before leaving, one of the suspects grabbed a wooden pickax handle to carry out the deed. A lone, nameless hobo with a few dollars in his pocket, walking along the tracks or asleep outside of the settlement, was ideal. Such victims wanted nothing to do with law enforcement and would not report they were the victim of a crime. The suspects knew they had until after seven in the morning or so, when the work crews left Bagdad, working their way eastbound.

Not having any luck, they likely climbed an elevated outcropping of lava that offered a perfect vantage point looking east and west. The suspects watched Otto leave Amboy alone and knew he was a good target. As Otto walked closer and closer, the suspects waited for the right time to leave their vantage point. Moving undetected and in tandem, they crouched down and made their way through the deep wash running between the lava and the railroad tracks. As Otto approached their hiding place, they stood up, and the suspect, armed with the pickax handle, raised the weapon over his head. He demanded Otto's money, while the second suspect blocked his path.

Otto refused, and the suspect swung the pickax handle and landed a glancing blow to his body. Like Moss, Otto fought back, and the two suspects struggled to subdue him. The fight continued with such ferocity it left the train tracks and spilled onto the desert ground, tearing it apart and crushing the creosotes. The unarmed suspect picked up a large rock and struck Otto in the head repeatedly until he stopped fighting. The second suspect stood up and finished Otto off with several strikes to his face and head with the pickax handle.

After taking the victim's money, the men looked up to see Clifton Hill bearing down on them from the west. In a panic, they tried to drag the body to the lava bed but were too tired, and Hill was getting closer. The exhausted suspects retreated to the lava and watched Hill discover the lifeless body. After looking at his watch, Hill looked around and quickly started towards Amboy to get help. They again tried to move the body but realized Hill would be back with more men, so they decided to split up and return to Bagdad with the fruits of the crime and blend in with the rest of the unemployed Mexicans.

Within a few hours, they learned about the discovery of the body and then, later, the arrest of Searcy. They were glad to hear Searcy had been arrested since it relieved them of any suspicion. The Mexicans watched the coroner's inquest at J. A. Stewart's saloon from a distance, made sure to stay away from the drunken proceedings, and were glad to see Searcy taken away. Life went on at Bagdad.

From the beginning, Searcy could not satisfactorily explain his whereabouts the day of the homicide. It is doubtful his hat blew off as he rode on top of the Pullman while it traveled into Danby. His story didn't make sense, because it's not likely he walked back several miles to look for his hat in the dark while the wind was blowing. Like A. J. Ballard, he hid and slept outside of Danby to avoid arrest for vagrancy, fare evasion, and the burglary warrant from Prescott. Both Ballard and Searcy decided to turn back and travel eastbound, away from the City of San Bernardino.

In the cooler months, there was a huge spike in arrests in San Bernardino for rail-related crimes, indicating the city's and county's low tolerance for tramps. It was common for tramps to be arrested for vagrancy or fare evasion and serve five to thirty days in county jail. Ballard probably warned Searcy to turn back to avoid arrest when they crossed paths outside of Bagdad. Deputies Keyes and Medlin both made these types of arrests at far-out settlements and Needles. After the local justice of the peace sentenced the arrestees, Keyes and Medlin would transport the suspects back to San Bernardino to complete their jail sentences. Part of the suspects' punishment was making them travel back the way they came to encourage them to stay out of San Bernardino. Once he arrived at Bagdad, Searcy made a point of staying out of view and turned back eastbound.

Obsessed with his self-professed celebrity status, T. F. Reardon could not accept the fact that Searcy may not be charged with murder due to the lack of evidence. He took it upon himself to look for more evidence and directed his work crew to move the outhouse, where he found currency in two separate locations. There was a five-dollar bill in a slit separating the men's and women's sections and two ten-dollar bills mixed in with the paper in the vault area. The argument by the prosecution was that this was money taken by Searcy during the robbery and hidden in the outhouse. Like Searcy's claim about his hat blowing off while he rode on top of the Pullman car, it didn't make sense. It seems more plausible the money in the slit was secreted by a railroad worker who had no other place to hide it. The other portion was also secreted somewhere in the outhouse and fell into the paper as the entire structure was moved by the work crew. The population of Danby was much smaller than Bagdad and consisted of transient laborers who slept in bunkhouses without any place to secure their money or valuables. An outhouse was the perfect place to hide these items while they were working away from the settlement.

The San Bernardino County criminal justice system was catapulted into an unstoppable momentum by T. F. Reardon's and G. W. Hess's self-initiated detective work. Deputy J. J. Arbios's lack of tracking expertise and footprint identification and Doctor McKechnie's questionable identification of blood corpuscles on Searcy's clothing solidified charges brought by the grand jury.

It's unknown if Gregorio Rede and Jose Nunez were the two suspects who murdered Joseph Otto. Still, the similarities between the murders of Joseph Otto and Johnie Moss are striking. Rede was seen with a black eye and a cut over his eye, which was most likely inflicted by Moss during the commission of the homicide. Searcy had no injuries, no torn clothing, no scratches, nothing that would result from a one-on-one homicide carried out at close-quarter contact resulting in death by blunt-force trauma. Moss, like Otto, was a lone traveler with a large amount of money whose body was dragged away from the scene of the crime. Both victims were murdered by blunt-force trauma to the head with a pickax or pickax handle. The gunshot wound most likely came as a result of Moss's initially slow death on the floor of Maceo's shack.

Moss would not have been missed by anyone in Bagdad if it were not for the fact that he left his horse behind the saloon. If it had not been for Clifton Hill, Joseph Otto's body would have been left in the desert for the animals to devour. The horse owned by Moss drew the suspicion of J. A. Stewart, who didn't want to be blamed for the missing man, as this was the third time his name would be associated with a violent death. As reported in the local media, Rede and Nunez were seen carrying the victim the night of murder on their "stalking" feet. This meant the suspects knew the footprints would be used to identify them. The same coverage reported the men tried to remove wood flooring covered in blood and to burn more incriminating evidence. They also wrapped the victim's head in a jacket belonging to Rede to prevent incriminating blood from marking the path where the body was taken.

Even after the cases of Searcy, Rede, and Nunez were adjudicated, the violence continued at Bagdad. On April 4, 1898, the *San Bernardino Daily Times* reported Sheriff Holcomb had brought Geronimo Delgardo in from Bagdad; Delgardo was under arrest for stabbing Abenico Gonzalez in the stomach during a drunken fight.[136] J. A. Stewart's saloon in Bagdad probably supplied the alcohol that fueled the drunken stabbing. On April 6, 1898, the *San Bernardino County Sun* reported Delgardo withdrew his plea from assault to kill, pleaded guilty to assault with a deadly weapon, and was sentenced to two years in San Quentin. The victim and Manual Paria were sworn in and prepared to testify against Delgardo.[137]

Louis James Searcy touched more people in his lifetime than anyone could have imagined, and his legal battle was the one case in so many careers that would never be forgotten. In the subsequent years, his attorneys went on to become a state and federal judge, a senator, a successful civil attorney, and a City of Los Angeles mayoral candidate. The case of the *State of California versus Louis James Searcy* would never be forgotten by any of them. Deputies J. L. Medlin, Frank Keyes, and J. J. Arbios would remember the drunken coroner's inquest and their testimony. It's a given that J. J. Arbios would never again testify about the positive identification of footprints belonging to a murder suspect.

Line 18 of page 548, the last page of the court transcripts—which had not been touched or read in over 115 years—captures the last words uttered on Searcy's behalf: "Defendant rests."

EPILOGUE

JAMES ALBERT STEWART (J. A. STEWART), THE MAYOR OF BAGDAD AND THE OLD MAN OF THE DESERT

By the turn of the century, Stewart's luck was running out and the sheriff's department was tired of his antics and flaunting of the law. In March 1900 the board of supervisors received a complaint about Stewart "selling alcohol right and left to anybody and everybody." Barely a year earlier, Stewart had been arrested for the same violation and paid a fifty-dollar fine but quickly returned to Bagdad to begin anew. An article from the *San Bernardino County Sun,* dated March 18, 1900, describes what happened next.

On March 14 Constables Charles More and Frank Holmes traveled to Bagdad with the intent of conducting an undercover investigation and arresting Stewart for the illegal sales of alcohol. The constables waited until the saloon closed and knocked on the back door, asking to buy a half-pint bottle of whiskey. Stewart was drunk and passed out and in no condition to serve the customer, so his sixty-year-old assistant, L. W. Greenwell, sold alcohol to the undercover constables. The constables soon realized Greenwell was not their target, so they waited and returned later to buy more whiskey. They once again knocked on the door, and at this time, Stewart got out of bed and sold the whiskey to the constables, who waited for him to return to bed after the sale. The armed men then quietly entered the closed saloon and surprised Stewart in his bed while covering him with their revolvers. A six-shooter lay on a table next to Stewart, ready to be used.[138]

The constables read Stewart the arrest warrant and took him and Greenwell on the train to San Bernardino to appear in court. While in county jail, Stewart described the circumstances of his arrest:

On the night before I was brought in, after all had retired and the house was closed, a party came to the back door. I was not in a condition to wait on him. I had a lodger that night, who volunteered his services to fill a half pint bottle. I took the visitor to be a hobo. In the morning, like a sneak thief, when I was alone in bed, the same party came to the door again and wanted a drink. I told him I was in no condition to wait on him being confined to my bed by sickness but under the circumstances I would do so. As far as their covering me with a six-shooter, it is a malicious lie. Holmes asked me if the gun on the table belonged to me. I told him it did but if he ever took possession of it I have no knowledge of it, and when More read the warrant to me, he claimed that a man by the name of Marks had sworn out the warrant. Anything to the contrary of this statement is a falsehood. J. A. Stewart[139]

Stewart begged for leniency, and Judge Thomas allowed him to plead guilty and pay a ninety-dollar fine. Greenwell was set free without charges being filed. The fine was a small cost of penance for the deaths and violence associated with Stewart and his saloon. R. E. Bledsoe, the father of B. F. Bledsoe, who had defended Searcy, represented Stewart in court, where Stewart promised to stop selling alcohol and get out of the illegal business. The same day of his court appearance in San Bernardino, his saloon was burned to the ground. By whom and for what reason it is not known, other than the fact that Stewart had plenty of enemies. The sheriff's department, the railroad company, the residents of Bagdad, the Mexicans, and the board of supervisors all had ample reasons to want Stewart and his saloon gone. Stewart may have been arrested twice for selling alcohol without a license, but it is unimaginable what crimes he committed or caused that went undetected.

By December 3, 1900, Stewart was fifty-seven years old, an alcoholic, a convict without family and friends, with no means to support himself. He drank his days away while living at Blake, another remote railroad settlement in the Mojave Desert, lamenting about the past and the grand old days of his saloon. It was too much for the "old man of the desert," and he took a clothesline and tried to hang himself from the gable of the roof of the building where he was residing. As he stood on top of a ladder, he kicked it out from under him, and the weight of his body caused the rope to snap. When he was found, his face was black and the rope was still tightly wrapped around his neck. The fall caused a deep cut on his chin. He was taken to the county hospital by Constable McNair, from the Vanderbilt Judicial Township, where he was kept pending an examination as to his sanity, which was caused by protracted drinking.[140] It was reported Stewart had eaten practically nothing since Thanksgiving Day.

"Stewart is now an old man, and he has lost all his property. In the palmy days of his reign at Bagdad, when his saloon was the most celebrated place in a radius of more than 100 miles, he had money galore, but misfortune has been bitter in later years."[141]

BENJAMIN FRANKLIN BLEDSOE
(B. F. BLEDSOE), DEFENSE ATTORNEY

Bledsoe was the standout attorney in the defense of Louis James Searcy. After the trial, he was elected judge of the Superior Court of San Bernardino County, in 1900, and was reelected in 1906. In 1914 President Wilson nominated him for United States district judge of the Southern District of California, and he was confirmed by the senate the same year. He resigned on March 24, 1925, to run for mayor of the City of Los Angeles but lost and resumed private practice with the law firm of Hill, Morgan, and Bledsoe in Los Angeles. He was married to Katherin Marvin Sheplar, and they had two daughters, Barbara and Frances Priscilla.

Some of his civic duties included involvement with the Board of Library Trustees, National Guard of California, University Club of Redlands, San Bernardino Chamber of Commerce, Benevolent and Protective Order of the Elks and the Native Sons of the Golden West. He was also the grand master of Masons of California, grand commander of Knights Templar, president of the Los Angeles Grand Opera Association, president of the Stanford Alumni Association, and an original board member of Forest Lawn Memorial Park. While at Stanford University, he became a close friend of former President Herbert Hoover, a friendship that lasted his entire life. B. F. Bledsoe died at his residence in Crestline in San Bernardino County on October 30, 1938, and is buried at Forest Lawn Memorial Park in Glendale, California.

HENRY MONTAGUE WILLIS
(H. M. WILLIS), DEFENSE ATTORNEY

After the trial, H. M. Willis returned to the Territory of Arizona to continue his legal practice. He served as a deputy district attorney in Maricopa County from 1898 to 1900 until his return to San Bernardino. Upon returning to San Bernardino, he was elected as the secretary for the Board of Trade, was involved in local politics, and joined civic-minded organizations.

In 1905 visitors from the San Bernardino Elks Lodge, including H. M. Willis, Judge B. F. Bledsoe, and Judge F. Oster, visited the Redlands Elks.[142] During this time, he engaged in private practice and handled a myriad of civil cases. He then served as a deputy district attorney from 1904 to 1906 until he was elected to the California State Senate, where he served two terms and continued to handle civil cases when not in session in Sacramento.

In 1930 Judge Willis officiated at his daughter's wedding at his Los Angeles home. He served as a Municipal and Superior Court judge and retired in 1958. He died at the age of eighty-eight in 1960.

GORDAN HALL, DEFENSE ATTORNEY

After the trial, Gordon Hall moved to San Francisco and opened a law firm, which turned into a lucrative legal practice. He developed a specialty in mining interests in Alaska and purchased valuable properties. He also owned a large ranch by Hanford. He died in August 1931 at the age of sixty, of a heart attack, while he was at home in Berkeley.

JOHN LEWIS MEDLIN (J. L. MEDLIN), CONSTABLE AND DEPUTY SHERIFF

After fifteen years as constable, Medlin was not placed on the Democratic ballot as a candidate, and his career as a constable at Daggett was over. In 1901 he was appointed as the constable for the township of Needles. Throughout his career, he would make arrests for vagrancy, fare evasion, burglary, and robbery and was well respected in Daggett and Needles. In 1911 he retired from law enforcement and moved to Los Angeles. He passed away in 1916. He is buried at the Inglewood Park Cemetery alongside his wife, Isola Medlin.

FRANK KEYES, DEPUTY SHERIFF

Frank Roselle Keyes returned to Needles after the trial, and the local community considered him a trustworthy and brave deputy who would sacrifice everything in the line of duty. He arrived at Needles in 1892 after spending three years as a deputy in Barstow. An example of his bravery occurred on May 31, 1893, when James Templeton and Pat Halpin started arguing inside a restaurant and Halpin left the establishment enraged. He quickly retrieved a revolver, returned to the area, and found Templeton seated in front of the F. R. Keyes and Co. Cigar Shop. Halpin immediately started to fire at Templeton and struck an innocent bystander in the back. He proceeded to fire four more times into the business, striking the front window and a jeweler's display case. Halpin then walked to the alley behind the business, looking for his victim, and about this time, Deputy Keyes exited his business. He ordered the suspect to drop the weapon, but he instead raised it in his direction. Deputy Keyes fired two rounds in rapid succession, mortally wounding Halpin. Frank Keyes served as the Needles's constable and deputy sheriff for seven years until his death in 1898, barely one year after the trial.

J. J. ARBIOS, DEPUTY SHERIFF

Joseph Jacob Arbios was a longtime resident and employee of San Bernardino County. He was a native of France and was born in the Pyrenees Mountains. He was eight years old when he moved to the United States with his parents and spoke five languages fluently. The family originally settled in Livermore and came to San Bernardino in 1880. In 1892 he was appointed as a deputy sheriff. He was elected as a constable of San Bernardino Township in 1894. He served in that capacity for twelve years, and after leaving law enforcement, he worked in various businesses, including mining and lumber in the vicinity of Big Bear and as a special investigator for the district attorney's office, court interpreter, and humane officer. Three years before his death, he was engaged in the sheep business in Fullerton. J. J. Arbios died at his residence in Los Angeles on April 28, 1920, at the age of sixty-three and is buried at the Mountain View Cemetery in San Bernardino.

ACKNOWLEDGMENTS

To my wife and the fun we had during our trips to the California State Archives in Sacramento, the city of Redding, and the cemeteries to pay homage to the characters that grace this story.

Many years ago, my best friend, Walt, encouraged me to go back to college and finish up my bachelor's degree, and I am forever grateful for his support. After completing my bachelor's, I was so enamored of education that I went on to obtain a master of arts degree in history while working full-time. During graduate school, I spent many evenings sitting in seminar classes with Dr. Choi Chatterjee, a wonderful professor of history at California State University, Los Angeles, who inspired me to always do better and made me feel at home in seminar classes filled with big-brained graduate students.

Upon retirement, I became involved in various historical societies and wrote short two-to-three-page articles on various desert-themed stories. I stumbled onto this story while looking for a one-to-two-page story about homicides in the remote railroad settlements at the turn of the nineteenth century. The story was buried in Newspapers.com, and a quick search of "Amboy" and "murder" yielded the murder of Joseph Otto and the arrest of Louis James Searcy. After reading a few newspaper accounts, I started to question the guilt of Searcy.

I contacted the San Bernardino County Assessor-Recorder-Clerk's office, which houses the county's historical documents, and I learned the assessor's office had the original case file containing motions, subpoenas, and the original handwritten guilty verdict. It shed some light on the case, but I needed more and learned there were documents at the California State Archives in Sacramento. On my first visit, a young archivist asked me exactly what I wanted to know about Searcy. I gave him a rambling response, and he disappeared and returned a short time later with a copy of the court transcripts, which had been untouched for over 115 years.

Special thanks to Joe De Kehoe, The author of *The Silence and Sun* for all his encouragement. He once said, "Steve, you are going to write a book about the desert, you just don't know it." Joe was right.

Special thanks to all the staff at the California State Archives, the California State Railroad Museum, the San Bernardino County Assessor-Recorder-Clerk's office, the San Bernardino County Museum, the San Bernardino Sheriff's Historical Society, the Needles Historical Society, and the Daggett Historical Society who all made this story possible. They are the keepers of our history. They were also extremely helpful and welcomed my research. And to my friends at the Twentynine Palms Historical Society where I serve as a board member.

APPENDIX I:
GRAVE SITES AT BAGDAD

During my research for *Four Miles East of Bagdad*, I had the opportunity to review the original logbooks for the San Bernardino County Coroner at the San Bernardino County Assessor-Recorder-Clerk's office. These enormous, original primary-source documents are available for the public to view and are a treasure trove of information about life and death in San Bernardino County during the turn of the nineteenth century. The coroner's entry into the logbook was sometimes accompanied by a file containing original documents and transcripts of the coroner's inquest. The documents include the names of the jurors and findings. Without these files I could not have written about the deaths of Jesus Lopez at the hands of J. A. Stewart or the murder of Johnie Moss

Bagdad remains as remote as it was in 1896, and the cemetery is cared for by visiting tourists and desert explorers. The names of the deceased remained a mystery, and the common myth was that the graves contained the bodies of Chinese railroad workers who died during a flu epidemic. During my research I discovered that the graveyard contains the bodies of three homicide victims. Jesus Lopez, Joseph Otto, and Johnie Moss are all resting at the lonely and remote graveyard. Their troubled souls and the stories of their violent demise were lost in time. To my amazement, I learned of eight additional forgotten souls buried at Bagdad, and the majority died as a direct result of working for the railroad at the remote settlement. Bentura Torres, laid to rest in 1911 at the age of eighteen months, is the youngest of the burials recorded. Not all deaths were reported to the county coroner, and the stories of the remaining graves will never be known.

Most likely, they were poor railroad workers without family or friends to care for their remains.

I was able to identify individuals who are buried at other settlements. The one that stands out the most is Mrs. Francisco Flores, thirty years old, who died on June 3, 1915, during childbirth at Danby. Mrs. Flores tried to give birth at one of the shacks at the settlement, and in June, the weather was already sweltering. There are at least three graves at Danby that sit up on a knoll looking down on the ghost settlement. One of the graves has a small fence around it, which seems to be most fitting for a mother and child buried in the desert.

Name/Age	Date	Cause of Death	Location Buried
James Woodbury (31)	03/07/93	Broken neck	Bagdad
Jesus Lopez (25)	01/29/96	Gunshot wound	Bagdad
Joseph Otto (48)	12/09/96	Beating	Bagdad
John Moss (42)	02/28/97	Homicide / wounds to face and shot in neck	Bagdad
Andres Tapia (27)	05/08/98	Fell from coal car breaking neck	Bagdad
O. Kuyama (39)	02/21/99	Apoplectic seizure	Bagdad
Robert Evergreen (26)	04/22/04	Run over by Sante Fe train	Bagdad

Name/Age	Date	Cause of Death	Location Buried
Bentura Torres (18 Months, 30 pounds)	09/23/11	Bainell trouble	Bagdad
William Butler (54)	01/16/13	Heart trouble	Bagdad
Samuel Landsburg (65)	06/25/24	Heat prostration (about 1.5 miles east of Bagdad)	Bagdad
Refurio Gustain (24)	02/5/25	Crushing injuries from accidentally falling from stock car while cars shunted to a sidetrack	Bagdad

NOTES

INTRODUCTION

[1] Testimony of Clifton Hill, 33.

[2] Thomas J. Schlereth, *Victorian America: Transformations in Everyday Life* (New York: Harper Collins Publishers, 1991), 1.

[3] Jeffrey Marcos Garcilazo, *Traqueros: Mexican Railroad Workers in the United States: 1870–1930* (Texas: UNT Press), 31.

[4] Jeremy Agnew, *Medicine in the Old West: A History, 1850–1900* (North Carolina: McFarland and Company, 2010), 172.

[5] Ibid., 57.

[6] Ibid., 58.

[7] Frank B. Latham, *The Panic of 1893: A Time of Strikes, Riots, Hobo Camps, Coxey's "Army." Starvation, Withering Droughts, and Fears of "Revolution"* (New York: Franklin Watts, 1971), introduction.

[8] Schlereth, 8.

[9] Ibid., 288.

[10] *San Bernardino County Board of Supervisors, 1855–2006* (California: County of San Bernardino, 2006), 1–5.

[11] Martha Stoebe, *San Bernardino County Museum: A Bicentennial County Commemorative Edition. Americas Largest County, Essay: The City of San Bernardino: County Seat* (Redlands: Allen-Greendale Publishers, 1974), 47.

[12] Jermey Agnew, *The Age of Dimes and Pulps: A History of Sensationalist Literature 1830–1860* (North Carolina: McFarland & Company, Inc., 2018), 3.

[13] David Myrick, *Railroads of Nevada and California* (Reno, Nevada: University of Nevada Press, 1992), 762–787.

CHAPTER I

[14] *Daily Courier*, Thursday, February 16, 1893, 3.

[15] *Needles Eye*, Saturday, April 22, 1893, 3.

[16] *Daily Facts*, Tuesday, September 18, 1894, 1.

[17] Physician's certificate, October 8, 1894.

[18] Coroner's Inquest of Jesus Lopez, January 29, 1896, courtesy of the San Bernardino County Assessor Recorder's Office, 1–84.

CHAPTER II

[19] Testimony of Conrad Stumpf, 283–298.

[20] "California, U.S., Voter Registers, 1866–1898," Ancestry.com.

[21] *Daily Courier*, November 17, 1886, 3.

[22] Testimony of G. W. Hess, 67.

CHAPTER III

[23] Testimony of Thomas Reardon, 250.

[24] "California, U.S., Voter Registers, 1898, and Sworn in Denver, Colorado, on October 15, 1887," Ancestry.com.

[25] Ms. Weaver later described the section house as a "boarding house" where workers could pay room and board.

[26] Ibid.

[27] Testimony of Reardon, 240–241.

[28] Testimony of Mrs. R. B. Weaver, 302–303.

[29] Testimony of Reardon, 244.

[30] Testimony of Mrs. R. B. Weaver, 306.

[31] Testimony of T. F. Reardon, 247.

[32] Testimony of J. L. Medlin, 176–195.

[33] Ibid.

[34] Testimony of J. J. Arbios, 216–217.

[35] Ibid., 122.

CHAPTER IV

[36] *Daily Courier*, January 12, 1892, 3.

[37] San Bernardino County Board of Supervisors' minutes, September 8, 1892.

[38] F. B. Daley would later be elected to district attorney in San Bernardino County.

[39] R. E. Bledsoe was the father of B. F. Bledsoe.

[40] *Weekly Courier*, September 17, 1892, 1.

[41] San Bernardino County Board of Supervisors' minutes, October 5, 1892, 10:00 a.m.

[42] Jeremy Agnew, *Medicine in the Old West: A History: 1850–1900* (North Carolina: McFarland and Company, 2010), 174.

[43] Opening statement of F. B. Daley.

[44] Testimony of G. W. Hess, 118.

[45] Testimony of Doctor Wesley Thompson, 437–449.

[46] *Prescott Weekly Journal Miner*, Arizona, January 12, 1898, 1.

[47] Testimony of A. J. Ballard, 309–333.

[48] Testimony of G. W. Hess, 118.

[49] Testimony of J. J. Arbios, 125.

[50] Testimony A. J. Ballard, 309–314.

[51] Testimony J. J. Arbios, 131–132.

[52] Ibid., 129–135.

[53] Coroner's inquest, December 8, 1896.

[54] Coroners logbook, December 9, 1896.

CHAPTER V

[55] *San Bernardino County Sun*, December 9, 1896, 1.

[56] *San Bernardino County Sun*, December 10, 1896, 4.

[57] Sprecher was elected as the San Bernardino County district attorney from 1903 to 1906.

[58] *San Bernardino County Sun*, December 13, 1896, 5.

CHAPTER VI

[59] Rodman Willoughby, *The History of the Bench and Bar of Southern California* (Los Angeles: Times Mirror Printing and Binding House, 1909), publisher's preface.

[60] Undated photo of Benjamin Franklin Bledsoe, Findagrave.com.

[61] Undated photo, Findagrave.com.

[62] "Henry M. Willis Sr.," Courtesy of San Bernardino Historical Society, 4.

[63] Accessgenealogy.com/california/biography-of-hon-henry-montague-willis.htm.

[64] "Elect Judge Henry M. Willis to the Superior Bench, Primary Election," advertisement, August 26.

[65] Willoughby, *The History of the Bench and Bar of Southern California*, 250–251.

[66] Edward Sanford Harrison, *Nome and Seward Peninsula: History, Description, Biographies, and Stories* (Metropolitan Press, 1905), 343.

[67] Willoughby, *The History of the Bench and Bar of Southern California*, 148.

[68] Ibid., 233.

[69] Ibid., 212.

CHAPTER VII

[70] "In the Superior Court of the County of San Bernardino, State of California, The People of the State of California, Plaintiffs vs. Louis J. Searcy," undated.

[71] Subpoena for Mr. Knuckles.

[72] "Defendant Exhibit 'A,'" letter on Sixth Avenue Hotel stationary, January 18, 1897, 1–2.

[73] "In the Superior Court of the County of San Bernardino, State of California, People of the State of California vs. Louis James Searcy, Motion for Continuance," February 23, 1897, 1–4.

[74] "Deposition of Witnesses," February 20, 1897, 1–13.

CHAPTER VIII

[75] "Strike" is a term used by hobos or tramps used to beg or trick proprietors at section houses into feeding them, either by a lie of being out of work or by exchanging labor for food. This could include chopping railroad ties for firewood or cleaning a kitchen at a Harvey House.

[76] "Working" was a term used to describe scamming a proprietor of a section house for food.

[77] Opening Statement of District Attorney F. B. Daley, 1–20.

CHAPTER IX

[78] Testimony of Louis James Searcy, 497.

[79] Otto Bettmann, *The Good Old Days—They Were Terrible* (New York: Random House, 1974), 142.

[80] Testimony of C. A. McKechnie, 390–405.

[81] *Weekly Sun*, March 6, 1897, 3.

CHAPTER X

[82] "People vs. Louis J. Searcy, Affiant of Benjamin Bledsoe on Motion for New Trial," March 15, 1897.

[83] *San Bernardino County Sun*, Tuesday, March 2, 1897, 7.

[84] *Redlands Daily Facts*, March 2, 1897, 1.

[85] *Weekly Sun*, March 6, 1897, 1.

[86] *San Bernardino County Sun*, March 11, 1897, 3.

[87] *San Bernardino County Sun*, April 21, 1897, 4.

[88] *San Bernardino County Sun*, April 25, 1897, 1.

[89] *San Bernardino County Sun*, April 27, 1897, 1.

[90] *Daily Times Index*, Tuesday, March 22, 1898, 5.

[91] *Daily Times Index*, April 4, 1898, 5.

[92] *Weekly Sun*, April 8, 1898, 6.

CHAPTER XI

[93] *Weekly Sun*, Saturday, April 10, 1897, 2.

[94] "Will Fight to the Finish," *Weekly Sun*, March 6, 1897.

[95] "In the Superior Court of California of the County of San Bernardino, People of the State of California vs. Louis James Searcy," March 15, 1897.

[96] "In the Superior Court of the County of San Bernardino, State of California, People vs. Louis James Searcy, Affidavit of Gordon Hall on Motion for new trial," March 15, 1897, 1–3.

[97] "In the Superior Court of the County of San Bernadino, State of California, People vs. Louis James Searcy," 1–3, signed by Joseph Bessant.

[98] "In the Superior Court of the County of San Bernadino, State of California, People vs. Louis James Searcy, Affidavit of Conrad Stumpf and Cliton Hill," March 29, 1897, 1–3.

[99] *San Bernardino County Sun*, Thursday, April 8, 1897, 4.

[100] *Weekly Sun*, Saturday, June 5, 1897, 4.

[101] *San Bernardino County Sun*, September 17, 1898, 3.

[102] *Evening Transcript*, October 6, 1898, 1.

CHAPTER XII

[103] William Seacrest, *Lawmen & Desperadoes: A Compendium of Noted, Early California Peace Officers, Badmen, and Outlaws* (Spokane, Washington: Arthur H. Clark, 1994), 17–18.

[104] San Quentin daily logbook, 21.

[105] John Halpern and David Blistein, *How an Ancient Flower Shaped and Poisoned Our World: Opium* (New York: Hachette Books, 2019), 176.

[106] San Quentin daily logbook, 177.

[107] Board State Prison Directors Meeting, book 5, 431–432.

[108] Board State Prison Directors Meeting, book 6, 33.

[109] Board State Prison Directors Meeting, book 7, 82.

[110] Ibid., 140.

[111] Board State Prison Directors Meeting, book 6, 59.

[112] San Quentin daily logbook, 79.

[113] Board State Prison Directors Meeting, book 5, 400.

[114] San Quentin daily logbook, 302.

[115] Ibid., 23.

[116] Ibid., 22.

[117] Board State Prison Directors Meeting, book 7, 230.

[118] "In the Superior Court of the State of California, County of San Bernardino. People of the State of California, Plaintiff vs. Louis J. Searcy," January 5, 1907.

[119] Sheldon L. Messinger, John E. Berecochea, David Rauma, and Richard A. Berk, "The Foundations of Parole in California," *Law and Society Review* 19, no. 1 (1985), 26–27.

[120] *San Bernardino County Sun*, July 17, 1908, 2.

CHAPTER XIII

[121] "I Had a Dream," the Long Ryders.

[122] Edward Petersen, *Redding the First Hundred Years* (Redding, California: North-Cal Printing and Litho, 1972), 12, 40.

[123] Letter to Governor James N. Gillet from the State Board of Prison Directors, July 30, 1910.

[124] *Searchlight*, August 6, 1911, 3.

[125] *Weekly Searchlight*. August 25, 1911, 3.

[126] *Record Searchlight*, January 25, 1915, 3.

[127] *Record Searchlight*, July 22, 1916, 3.

[128] *Shasta Courier*, May 24, 1918, 1.

[129] *Shasta Courier*, March 25, 1919, 4.

[130] *Record Searchlight*, August 16, 1919, 3.

[131] *Record Searchlight*, November 10, 1923, 1.

[132] *Sacramento Bee*, April 25, 1923, 9.

[133] *Record Searchlight*, April 8, 1930, 6.

[134] *Record Searchlight*, January 27, 1934, 1.

[135] *Record Searchlight*, January 29, 1934, 6.

[136] *San Bernardino County Sun*, April 6, 1898, 4.

[137] *Weekly Sun*, April 8, 1898, 6.

EPILOGUE

[138] *San Bernardino County Sun*, Sunday, March 18, 1900, 8.

[139] *Evening Transcript*, March 16, 1900, 3.

[140] *Daily Times Index*, Thursday, December 5, 1901, 1.

[141] *San Bernardino County Sun*, Friday, December 6, 1901, 8.

[142] *Weekly Sun*, October 13, 1905, 3.

BIBLIOGRAPHY

Agnew, Jeremy. *Medicine in the Old West: A History, 1850–1900.* North Carolina: McFarland and Company, 2010.

Agnew, Jermey. *The Age of Dimes and Pulps: A History of Sensationalist Literature 1830–1860.* North Carolina: McFarland and Company, 2018.

Bettmann, Otto. *The Good Old Days—They Were Terrible.* New York: Random House, 1974.

San Bernardino County Board of Supervisors, 1855–2006. California: County of San Bernardino, 2006.

Garcilazo, Jeffray Marcos. *Traqueros: Mexican Railroad Workers in the United States: 1870–1930.* Texas: UNT Press, 2012.

Halpern, John and David Blistein. *How an Ancient Flower Shaped and Poisoned Our World: Opium.* New York: Hachette Books, 2019.

Latham, Frank B. *The Panic of 1893: A Time of Strikes, Riots, Hobo Camps, Coxey's "Army." Starvation, Withering Droughts, and Fears of "Revolution."* New York: Franklin Watts, 1971.

Myrick, David. *Railroads of Nevada and California.* Reno, Nevada: University of Nevada Press, 1992.

Petersen, Edward. *Redding the First Hundred Years.* Redding, California: North-Cal Printing and Litho, 1972.

Schlereth, Thomas J. *Victorian America: Transformations in Everyday Life.* New York: Harper Collins Publishers, 1991.

Stoebe, Martha. *San Bernardino County Museum: A Bicentennial County Commemorative Edition. Americas Largest County, Essay: The City of San Bernardino: County Seat.* Redlands: Allen-Greendale Publishers, 1974.